Structures and forces
Stage 3

A Unit for teachers

Published for the Schools Council by
Macdonald Educational, London and Milwaukee

First published in Great Britain 1973 by
Macdonald Educational Ltd
Holywell House, Worship Street
London EC2A 2EN

Macdonald-Raintree Inc.
205 W. Highland Avenue
Milwaukee, Wisconsin 53203

Reprinted 1974 (with amendments), 1980

ISBN 0 356 04107 7

Library of Congress Catalog Card Number
77-82991

The chief author of this book is:

Albert James   Deputy Project Director

The other members of the Science 5/13 team are:

Len Ennever   Project Director

Wynne Harlen   Evaluator

Sheila Parker
Don Radford
Roy Richards
Mary Horn

Made and printed by Waterlow (Dunstable) Limited

General preface

'Science 5/13' is a project sponsored jointly by the Schools Council, the Nuffield Foundation and the Scottish Education Department, and based at the University of Bristol School of Education. It aims at helping teachers to help children between the ages of five and thirteen years to learn science through first-hand experience using a variety of methods.

The Project produces books that comprise Units dealing with subject areas in which children are likely to conduct investigations. Some of these Units are supported by books of background information. The Units are linked by objectives that the Project team hopes children will attain through their work. The aims of the Project are explained in a general guide for teachers called *With objectives in mind* which contains the Project's guide to Objectives for children learning science, reprinted at the back of each Unit.

Acknowledgements

Metrication

The Project is deeply grateful to its many friends: to the local education authorities who have helped us work in their areas, to those of their staff who, acting as area representatives, have borne the heavy brunt of administering our trials, and to the teachers, heads and wardens who have been generous without stint in working with their children on our materials. The books we have written drew substance from the work they did for us, and it was through their critical appraisal that our materials reached their present form. For guidance, we had our sponsors, our Consultative Committee and, for support, in all our working, the University of Bristol. To all of them we acknowledge our many debts; their help has been invaluable.

This has given us a great deal to think about. We have been given much good advice by well-informed friends, and we have consulted many reports by learned bodies. Following the advice and the reports whenever possible we have expressed quantities in metric units with Imperial units afterwards in square brackets if it seemed useful to state them so.

There are, however, some cases to which the recommendations are difficult to apply. For instance we have difficulty with units such as miles per hour (which has statutory force in this country) and with Imperial units that are still in current use for common commodities and, as far as we know, liable to remain so for some time. In these cases we have tried to use our common sense and, in order to make statements that are both accurate and helpful to teachers we have quoted Imperial measures followed by the appropriate metric equivalents in square brackets if it seemed sensible to give them.

Where we have quoted statements made by children, or given illustrations that are children's work, we have left unaltered the units in which the children worked—in any case some of these units were arbitrary.

Contents

Illustration acknowledgements:

The publishers gratefully acknowledge the help given by the
following in supplying photographs on the pages indicated:

Autocar, 32
The Associated Press Limited, 13
Barnaby's Picture Library, 12, 36, 55, 62, 77
British Aircraft Corporation Ltd, 5
British Leyland Motor Corporation Ltd, 61
Cement and Concrete Association, 66, 67
Central Electricity Generating Board, 48
Dunlop Ltd, 26
Ford Motor Company Ltd, 32
Highway Code by permission of the Controller of Her Majesty's
Stationery Office, 27
James B. Wright, 20, 39
The Mansell Collection, 17
Natural History Photographic Agency, 18
Road Research Laboratory, 28, 63
The Science Museum, London, 6, 26
Smiths Industries Limited, 23

Line drawings by The Garden Studio: Corinne Clark

Cover design by Peter Gauld

Introduction

The children for whom it is intended

This Unit is related to a stage in children's mental development characterised by ability to think abstractly. We call it Stage 3. This does not mean that a child having reached this stage is going to be given work involving abstract thinking all the time. Even the ablest minds in the greatest universities derive much help in their work from such activities as dabbling with sand and water in the cellars. It is still felt to be essential that the work is approached from *experience* as at earlier levels, but the ability to generalise (for example about forces causing accelerations) can now be used with powerful effect.

The work then is not for a particular age of child, a particular form, class or year of a school or indeed for any particular type of school organisation, but for a stage in the development of a child. Since in any particular group of children there will probably be some at each of several different stages, it will be necessary to organise rooms, materials and methods of teaching to suit this divergence and, in addition to allow for the very different *rates* of development of individuals.

It should be understood that this Unit does not represent a 'course' or a text to work steadily through from beginning to end, even though it has an ordered arrangement of the material.

Many teachers will want to select from the Unit, perhaps, for example, to construct their own work-cards to suit their rooms, school environment, time at their disposal and how that time is split up; but more especially to suit the particular group of children concerned, their interest and rate of development. If the teacher's objectives are clearly enough in mind there are several paths to choose from.

Experience leading to simplified generalisations

The great thing about a child who has reached what we have called Stage 3 is that a simplified generalisation from experience can now be seen as a useful tool to take thinking further. If the earth pulls the apple, it also pulls the moon and if we can find some rule about things falling we might be able to work out why the moon doesn't fall back to earth but goes round and round. It would still be a pity, however, if the fact was missed that in practice things do *not* all fall at the same rate but that air resistance frequently causes very interesting things to happen. Flight and friction come before Fletcher's Trolley!

Practical work might give an experience of, say, different tensile strengths. An aim would no doubt be to reach some mathematical generalisation as a useful simplification of a rough pattern seen experimentally, so one would hope to finish up with a 'law'. But also (and this is very important) one would hope to have a great deal of understanding of its limitations (in this case perhaps about elastic limits).

Too often in the past the 'law' has been taught *first*, with a demonstration of its 'truth' (usually taking a very special case in order to demonstrate it), followed by numerical examples to 'drive it home'. Good examination technique perhaps, but bad science. This is simply putting the mathematical cart before the scientific horse. (Is the situation similar perhaps, to the over-anxiety at an earlier stage to teach children to

1

read, resulting often in the use of methods which can only inhibit the later imaginative use of language?)

The content of the Unit

Is there a general framework of content for science teaching into which the material of this Unit fits?

In the primary stages there is no need for a picture of science in any completeness. The excitement of observation and discovery activities are often sufficient reward in themselves. What we feel has to be done for Stage 3 is to give some picture of a pattern to which the work is leading. The children who have reached this Stage begin to look for some logical wholeness in life, and as knowledge of the facts of science increases, organisation of it begins to be imperative. But there is so much science to learn. What could possibly be left out? It would be easy to become lost in all the difficulties of syllabus writing.

It seems that a good approach for the middle years of schooling is to sort out the major important areas of science which can be taught in a wide simple way, thus forming a basis, equally sound both for those who will follow on with a more advanced academic study of science, and for those who will not. The following list of seven areas is an attempt to do this. It was made by collecting together statements of content from many courses and projects in science which are appropriate to the stages of children's development we are considering and which are already widely accepted and used. These were grouped by looking for common main ideas rather than separate items of knowledge under different headings:

1. The environment
Conditions on earth and in space.

Simple geology and oceanology.

The environment as a source of materials.

Weather and climate.

Simple astronomy.

2. The wealth and nature of plant and animal life
The main differences in environments for living.

Life histories of selected animals and plants (arising from the study of the environment rather than selection based on the traditional evolutionary sequence); adaptation.

3. Man and his place in the order of things
Man as a social and intelligent animal.

Conservation and exploitation.

Pests and their control.

Pollution.

Food: health.

4. Differences, similarities and patterns
Grouping materials according to properties.

Grouping plants and animals according to their observable characteristics and behaviour.

Classification as an aid to scientific thinking.

5. Interaction and change
Effecting changes and controlling changes.

The main processes which enable organisms to exist.

The idea that evolution took place and is continuing.

Stability and instability in systems.

Equilibrium, force and motion.

Material changes. Some effects of heat and electricity. Chemical interaction. Change of state.

Rates of change.

6. Energy changes which accompany material changes
Forms of energy. Energy and work.

Sources of energy.

Energy conversions (including those in living things).

Energy chains. Energy storage.

The electro-magnetic energy spectrum.

7. The organisation of matter
The way larger organisms and objects are made from smaller parts.

The particulate nature of things.

Structure: organisms, mechanical structures, matter.

Levels of organisation.

Pattern. Structures made from repeating units.

Shape related to purpose.

Conditions controlling size. Size and volume, size and weight, size and surface area, size and strength.

Measurements. Degrees of accuracy.

This classification shows simply an over-all picture of what all children might have sampled by the age of thirteen, but it cannot be over-emphasised that the main factor which will decide both how much they can cover and at what depth will be decided by the stage of mental development they have reached.

The material in the two *Structures and forces* Units (this one and that for Stages 1 and 2) will be found, at different levels, to fit into a number of the main areas described above.

In the Unit *Structures and forces, Stages 1 & 2*, the forces met with were always balanced and the structures in which they acted did not move. We shall look at these tension and compression forces again towards the end of the present Unit along with some further ideas about structure, but the first part concerns forces which make things move.

Forces moving things

Power

A good way of making a start is to look at some of the powerful things we use.

What is the most powerful car you could buy?

What is the power of a diesel locomotive and the QE2?

What horsepower is needed for a super oil tanker?

How powerful are space rockets and jet planes?

How much power does an electricity power station turn out and how does a coal-burning plant compare with a nuclear station?

What is the power of a nuclear bomb?

A look at motoring magazines will provide facts about the brake horsepower of cars (bhp) and some graph-charts may be made. All that is needed at this point is a comparison, and the unit, bhp, may be taken for granted, although it is an interesting story how the first firms to buy the early steam engines needed to compare the power of them with that of horses, which is what they were used to. Experiments were made with many horses to see how fast they could pull weights up a well shaft. On the average, a horse could lift 550 pounds-weight one foot per second and so this was called one horsepower. The term *brake* horsepower indicates that nowadays engines are tested against the pull of a brake instead of against the pull of gravity.

This practical and colourful unit may take some time

to die out under metrication. It will be interesting to note when manufacturers begin to quote the power of cars in kilowatts.

The 'power' of space rockets and jet planes is usually given as the amount of thrust they produce. This is a *force* and not power, if we are going to stick to a strict definition, but for the time being let us use the word 'power' in an everyday sort of way. The initial static thrust of Apollo 16 was over seven million pounds force. Children can collect from the news and aeronautical magazines the latest information about Concorde's engines, jumbo jets and the vertical take-off planes for example. They may look at the plates on railway diesel-electric engines. (A typical one reads: Weight 117 tons, Tractive Force 60 tons.)

An electricity power station's output is usually measured

in *megawatts* (mega = million).

Again there is no need to dwell on the meaning of the units used. In the case of power stations one might compare the number of one-bar electric fires which they would work, each taking 1000 watts (1 kilowatt), or the number of 100-watt bulbs they would light.

The power of nuclear weapons is usually spoken of in megatons of the 'old' explosive, TNT; a unit (fortunately) quite inconceivable to most of us.

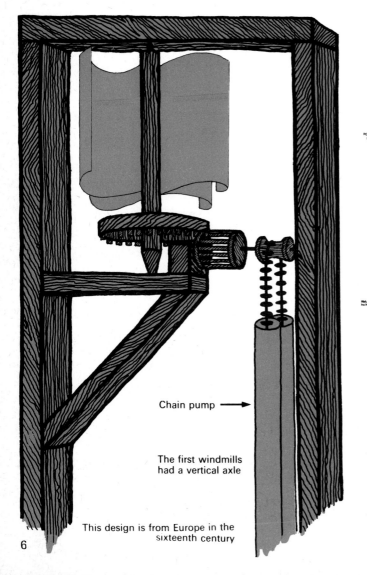

Chain pump →

The first windmills had a vertical axle

This design is from Europe in the sixteenth century

6

DUTCH WIND DRIVEN SCOOP WHEEL
EARLY 18TH CENTURY

ELEVATION
with
PORTION OF COVERING & PART OF
EARTH & BRICKWORK REMOVED

PART PLAN SHOWING LOWER PORTION OF MILL
SECTION ON AA

The history of the development of power appeals to some children. They often like to make models of early machinery especially, perhaps, windmills and water-wheels. The best of these may be big enough actually to drive, say, a dynamo to light bulbs. Some schools are lucky enough to have fast-flowing streams near to them for providing water power.

The changes brought about by the steam engine and the internal combustion engine make a very remarkable story. Some children would like to spend time finding out how they work, possibly investigating model steam engines, and the parts of a real car or motorcycle engine.

The need to conserve fuel and the possibilities of nuclear power will make interesting discussion topics.

Energy

Where does all the 'power' come from? In most cases some fuel is burned, in others the energy from moving water or moving wind is used.

Energy is a common everyday word. Advertisements claim that breakfast foods give it to us and we are all well aware whether we have it or are lacking it.

Energy is simply the ability to do work.

To get work done, energy has to be changed from one form to another. For example, we get energy out of a lump of coal by burning it in air. We have changed chemical energy to heat which can be used. We ourselves can do work because our bodies, by complicated biochemical changes, convert the energy in the food we eat to movement in our muscles.

And where do lumps of coal and the food we eat get *their* energy from? Almost all energy chains when traced backwards lead to the sun, which pours out heat and light continuously produced from changes in the nuclei of hydrogen atoms as huge numbers of them collide at furious speeds.

On the following pages are some pleasant small experiments about energy changes. The idea is to provide children with experiences through which they may gradually begin to build up a concept of energy. They might be asked to devise further interesting

illustrations of energy changes themselves and usually enjoy the challenge to their imagination.

The experiments will create a need for terms describing different forms of energy and the following will be useful:

a. Potential energy (energy due to position or state)

We can get work done by objects which are raised up, simply by letting them fall. Material which is strained, such as a wound-up spring or a stretched piece of rubber also has potential energy.

b. Kinetic energy (energy due to movement)

We can get work done by an object which is moving either along a line or rotating.

Strictly speaking, all forms of energy can be collected under the above two headings but at the level at which we are working it is convenient to use the following as well:

c. Heat energy

We can get work done by objects which are hotter than their surroundings.

Many series of energy changes end up by very slightly warming up the surroundings.

d. Chemical energy (produced or used up in chemical changes)

Examples are the energy in petrol and in an electric battery.

e. Electrical energy (produced or used when an electrical current flows)

f. Magnetic energy

g. Energy in radio waves, infra-red waves, light waves, X-rays.

Energy is transferred by these waves without any material thing moving.

h. Sound energy

The energy in sound waves is particularly evident when planes 'break the sound barrier' and in ultrasonics.

i. Nuclear energy (from the sun or a nuclear power station).

Experiences with energy changes

1. What energy changes take place when you:

Lift a parcel of books on to a shelf?

Drop a brick on the floor?

Play with a yo-yo?

Blow up a balloon and release it?

Blow up a paper bag and burst it?

Shoot an arrow from a bow into a target?

Fly a kite, a glider or a model plane?

Use a battery to light a bulb or ring a bell?

Rub a pen on cloth and lift a small piece of paper with it?

Let a Slinky spring move down some steps? (Why doesn't it stop after one step?)

Use a photographic exposure-meter?

Take a photograph by daylight or using a flash bulb?

2. Wind up clockwork toys and the alarm mechanism of an old clock which can be taken to pieces. Watch what happens to the spring as the toys work and the alarm rings. How does a spring store up energy and let it go again? Where did the energy come from? How far will the clockwork car run and how long does the alarm ring when the spring is

Fully wound?
Half wound?

How did you decide what was 'half wound'?

3. Wind up a bobbin tractor and run it along the table. How is the driving energy stored up? Have a competition to devise the most powerful model. What are the variables? Apart from using different rubber bands, you can change the material from which you make the tractor, the length of the 'arm' and the size of the whole thing. How big a one can you make? Does bigger always mean better or is there a best size?

How do you decide which is most powerful? Do you just measure distance travelled or do you take account of weight and speed?

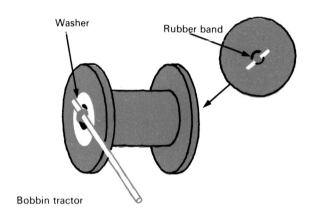

Washer · Rubber band

Bobbin tractor

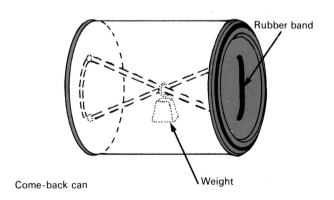

Rubber band

Come-back can · Weight

Roll the can along the floor for a few yards. What happens? Look inside the can to find out why. How far will the can roll back on its stored up energy? Where has the energy gone to when it stops?

In many of these experiments we seem to be using up energy but this is not so. We often finish with heat energy which warms the atmosphere up a little and is no use to us, but in fact we assume that the total amount of energy in the universe is always the same, so energy does not get used up but simply changes its form.

4. Put a small amount of water at room temperature in a container and note its temperature. Stir vigorously, eg with an egg whisk, for ten minutes and take the temperature again. Continue taking temperature readings for further ten-minute whiskings. Make a graph. How do you explain the result in terms of energy?

The rise in temperature is not very dramatic. It helps to have a well-insulated container, a small amount of water and a team to do the work. The experiment has been enjoyed by a whole class 'passing it round' but often children are disappointed.

Try taking the temperatures of liquids being stirred in a kitchen mixer. One mixer was found to raise the temperature of two cups full of water [about 400 ml] by 0·25°C per minute. A liquidiser warms the same amount by about 0·4° C per minute.

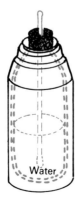

Water

Alternatively, shake some water in a vacuum flask fitted with a cork and thermometer as shown and make a graph of the temperature taken every ten minutes.

Does the volume of water used have any effect?

Other ways of demonstrating the production of heat from kinetic energy are:

To drill a hole in metal.

To hammer a nail vigorously into a piece of hard wood.

To rub a piece of metal vigorously on a cloth for a minute.

To bend a piece of wire (eg a paper-clip) rapidly backwards and forwards.

In each case the rise in temperature can be felt with the fingers.

Car tyres feel quite hot after a run. Where has this heat come from?

A school possessing a galvanometer or micro-ammeter can connect a simple thermocouple to it as shown in the diagram.

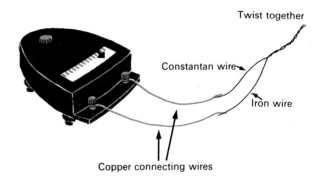

Galvanometer

Twist together

Constantan wire

Iron wire

Copper connecting wires

The junction of the wires may be heated by the fingers or with a match, heat being converted directly to electrical energy.

It is possible to get a deflection of the pointer by hammering the junction. (Note: Not on the same table as the galvanometer!)

5. Heat a tin lid until it is almost red hot. Then turn off the heater and drop on the lid a match-head wrapped tightly in foil from cigarettes or chocolate. Stand well back. Make a list of all the energy changes which take place.

A book-match wrapped in foil and heated at the head end will make a nice rocket.

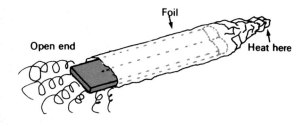

6. Hold a piece of dowel rod vertically with ring magnets repelling one another as shown.

Press down the top magnet to push them all together

The energy used to do this is stored in the magnetic field. Release the top magnet. What happens to the stored energy?

7. The 'Noddy peg'

Half of a 20-cm length of stiff wire is wound round a pencil and then slipped over a long dowel rod of slightly smaller diameter.

Gently press down on the clothes peg and then release it. What changes of energy take place?

Quite apart from questions about energy, this amusing toy has evoked some interesting experimental work when the variables concerned have been considered.

What difference is made by altering the following:

The position of the peg on the wire?

The weight of the peg?

The thickness of the wire?

The material of the wire?

The diameter of the coil?

The tightness or openness of the coil?

The even or uneven nature of the coil?

The material of the vertical rod?

The diameter of the vertical rod?

How are these factors related to:

a. The time taken to fall a given height?

b. The number of bounces?

8. Connect together two low-resistance telephone earpieces with a long length of flexible wire, and by speaking and listening alternately, use them to telephone from room to room.

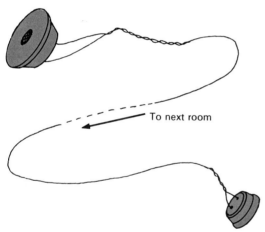

Make a list of all the energy changes which take place.

A very similar energy cycle may be set up as shown below. Each unit of spring, magnet and coil must be exactly alike, ie they must be 'tuned', The magnets should be strong ones. They adhere by their own magnetism to the hacksaw blades which must be adjusted to allow the magnets to rise and fall freely within the coils. To do this, packing with paper is usually required at the point shown in the drawing.

If one blade is set oscillating, the other responds with the same movement.

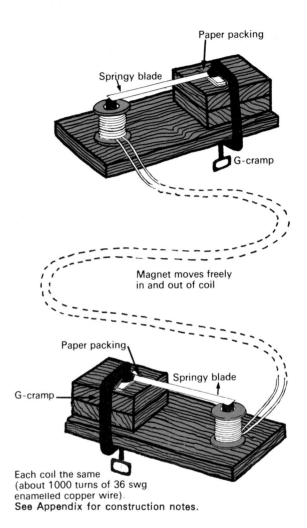

Each coil the same (about 1000 turns of 36 swg enamelled copper wire). **See Appendix for construction notes.**

9. Two exactly similar toy cars with 'inertia motors' (fly-wheels) may be obtained. The mechanism is removed from one so that it runs freely, but its weight is made up to that of the other car with Plasticine. Start the cars together at the top of a slope.

How do they run differently? Do they each start with the same amount of energy? How is it used differently?

10. Some children may bring in an interesting toy called Crookes's radiometer.* (They can be bought from several stores and toy departments. See Appendix.)

It is fascinating to see heat energy converted to energy of movement in the vanes.

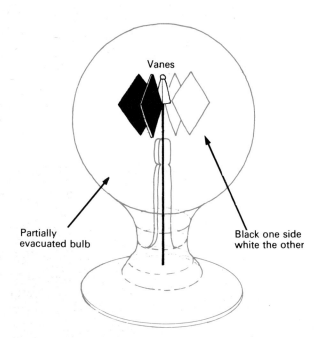

Vanes

Partially evacuated bulb

Black one side white the other

The explanation is difficult and does not really need to be considered at this stage, but some advanced children might like to think about it. One must know, or find out, that black surfaces absorb radiation more effectively than white ones. (This is very easy to do. One thermometer should be placed under a piece of black paper and another under a piece of white paper in the sun or in the light from an electric bulb.)

Thus the black side of the vanes becomes warmer than the other side. Molecules of air left in the bulb are shot from the black surfaces more vigorously than from the white surfaces causing the vanes to be pushed in the opposite direction.

*Sir William Crookes, President of the Royal Society 1913–16

Discussions

While these practical experiences are going on, discussions should constantly arise about energy changes met with in everyday life and in the news.

Perhaps diagrams and wall charts about these could be made. Some examples of topics might be:

Driving a car. (Where has all the energy in the petrol gone when we get back home after a drive?)

Going up and down a tall building in a lift.

Sailing a yacht.

Riding a surf-board.

Watching television.

Standing in the rain.

The great size of energy change in natural phenomena such as avalanches, earthquakes, volcanoes, typhoons, thunder and lightning.

How much energy is needed to make it rain *(left)* ?
A spectacular energy change; Mount Etna erupting in May 1971 *(below)*

Doing work

A collection may be made of small model motors and engines which a group of children can bring. (For the sake of safety and convenience it may be best to exclude power tools and larger motors worked directly from the mains.)

How can we find how much power the motors have?

Which is the most powerful of them all?

One suggestion will certainly be to see what weight they will lift.

Electric motors may be simply mounted as shown and tests made to see how many marbles each will just lift from the floor. (See Appendix for a range of motors which may be bought.)

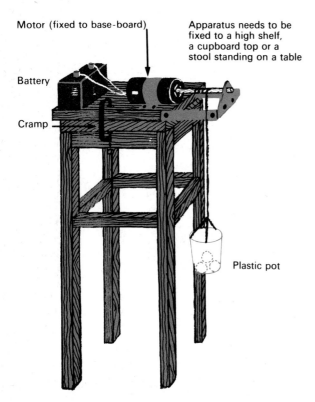

Motor (fixed to base-board)

Apparatus needs to be fixed to a high shelf, a cupboard top or a stool standing on a table

Battery

Cramp

Plastic pot

This will soon be found to be a difficult and unsatisfactory sort of test. Can we improve it? Let us bring *time* into it.

Take the time with a stop-watch for a motor to wind up the plastic pot alone from the floor to the level of the table. Then measure the time with one marble in the pot, two marbles, three marbles and so on. (Of course use paper clips, nails or washers as standard weights if they are more convenient.)

Make a graph of number of marbles against time. Can you find out if the diameter of the motor shaft makes a difference? Repeat the test with other motors. Draw all the graphs with the same axes. How do the graphs show the different powers of the motors at a glance?

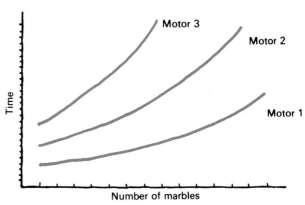

Motor 3

Motor 2

Motor 1

Time

Number of marbles

Starting with a familiar, everyday word, *power*, we have built up experiences which show a need to be more precise about how it is measured.

Power is measured by the rate of doing work, ie by how much work is done per second or per minute, etc. The more power we have the faster we can do work. (Do you remember how the size of the unit 'one horsepower' was decided?)

It is obvious that there is also a need to be more precise about the word *work*.

Work is done when a force moves, and the amount of work is measured by the size of the force times the distance it moves.

Inventing force-measurers

2. Using the pusher-puller described in the Unit for Stages 1 and 2 and drawn below.

Piece of broomstick or dowel

Tube (eg from old TV aerial)

Elastic or spring

Screw

Pusher-puller

The force in our experiments with the motors was caused by the earth's gravity pulling on some marbles, giving them weight (which is a force). There are many other kinds of forces. How can they be measured? One may, for example, push into clay or Plasticine; squeeze a balloon; bend a strip of wood, metal or plastic; stretch elastic or a spring; or twist a wire. (At present concentrate on the fact that forces may deform materials. Later, other ways of measuring force will be seen.)

A group of children can set about seeing how many different force measurers they can invent and using them to measure many common pushes and pulls, for example, those required to turn handles and knobs, close doors or lift latches. They could find the pull of magnets on iron and the effect of one magnet on another.

Which measurer is most convenient?

Do they give the same results every time they are tested with the same force?

Do they always come back to zero?

Do they give the same results as each other when comparing the same forces?

A teacher should see what inventive skill children have and let them enjoy trying a variety of their own ideas before introducing the following activities more formally.

1. Stretching elastic. Almost any elastic band will do. Square section, 'catapult elastic' can be bought (see Appendix). Shirring elastic, used in needlework, is very useful.

3. Stretching a spiral spring.

4. Compressing a spiral spring, eg a furniture spring.

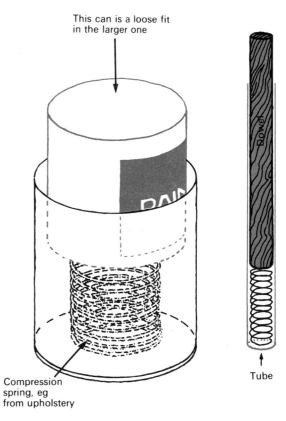

This can is a loose fit in the larger one

Dowel

Compression spring, eg from upholstery

Tube

5. Compressing air, eg in a bicycle pump in which the handle has been pulled out before sealing up the air hole, or in a plastic syringe (see Appendix).

6. Twisting a rubber tube or bending a wire.

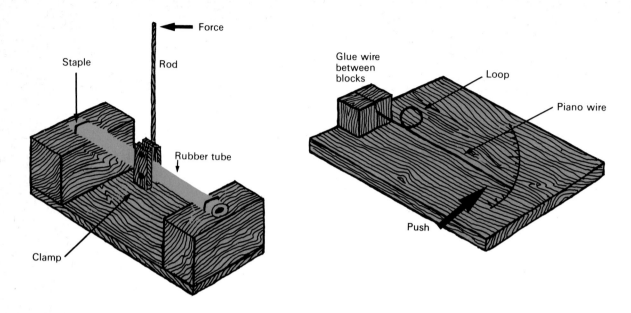

7. Bending strips of material. Almost anything may be used, eg a long eraser or a ruler.

A most useful force-measurer can be made from a hacksaw blade, as shown on the left.

Several should be made, using different lengths of hacksaw blade to give a range of forces and other kinds of blades and flexible materials could be used. Don't forget to paint a number on each one so that it can be found to use again if necessary.

Scales to measure with
On the force-measurers, some kind of scale will be needed.

1. At first all that is necessary is a blank card. For example with the hacksaw blade instrument, the size of a force can be shown by making a pencil mark where the end of the blade comes to. Alternatively, a set of marks, made quite arbitrarily, at equal distances will be useful.

2. The situation will soon arise where children will

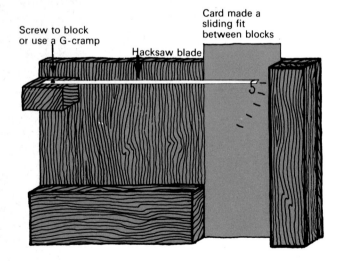

want to compare each others measurers. Then the need for a *standard* unit of force will arise. The group should agree together on something simple. It could be the weight of a ball-bearing, a marble, a large washer or a certain size nail for example; something easily available. A separate card for all the agreed units can be made to slip into each hacksaw blade force-meter. Mark the cards with the same reference number as the meter.

A good challenge at this point is to invent measurers for very small forces. Fine wire will probably have to replace the hacksaw blade and the unit of force might now be a milk bottle top, a paper-clip, one square inch of paper, or one centimetre of drinking straw.

3. Children who have reached Stage 3 will soon want to know the *real* unit used, and a teacher can have meters ready marked in *newtons*. This can be done by remembering that 1 kilogram weight = 9·8 newtons. It might be accurate enough at this stage to reckon a newton as equal to 100 gram weight.

This conversion should not be taught. How a newton comes to be worked out will be seen later on. At this point it is presented simply as the standard unit of force and is as easy to accept as degrees on a thermometer or centimetres on a ruler.

Common pushes and pulls in a school can now be measured by different measurers in newtons and average results agreed on and charted.

Starting, keeping going and stopping

Things do not move by themselves, they stay put unless pushed or pulled by a force. If we leave a book on a table one night and in the morning find it on the floor, we know someone has pushed it. (There might have been an earthquake or a mighty wind, but no doubt in that case there would have been additional evidence.) It was by extending this kind of everyday experience into the realm of what might be which caused our ancestors to imagine that winds were caused by the blowing of giants from the four corners

Part of an engraving by Albrecht Dürer (1471-1528)

of the earth, and to invent a wonderful hierarchy of angels, archangels, principalities and powers in order to move the sun, moon, planets and stars.

A good way to start this section would be to collect lists of things which move (and what doesn't) and to think out where the forces come from which move them. In most cases the answer will be easy to see but not always. What force makes a plant grow, opens a

17

Daisies in daylight and at dusk

daisy's petals with the daylight and closes them at dusk, raises water to the top of a tree or moves blood round an animal's body? And if angels and archangels do seem a bit far-fetched, what *does* turn the world round and why does the universe keep moving? What forces keep electrons spinning round the nucleus of an atom?

Does your house move? The fact that it is spinning rapidly and travelling in orbit round the sun along with the rest of the earth is interesting, especially if one works out the speed of each of these motions. Then, of course, the sun is rapidly spinning around our galaxy with the thousands of millions of other stars which go to make it, and the whole galaxy (the Milky Way) is probably drifting through space. All movement is relative. We really have to say each time what we are taking to be fixed and stationary. For everything in this book we will assume the earth to be still!

Force is needed to start and stop: Inertia

Stationary objects resist moving or, if they are moving already, they resist stopping. They have *inertia* (the word simply means 'laziness'). We have a good deal of experience of the inertia of our own bodies (quite apart from the kind which makes us unwilling to get up in the morning). A rapidly starting car or plane drives us back hard into our seat and we need seat belts to prevent us being thrown violently forward in the event of a rapid stop. Standing passengers in a bus have inertia and tend to keep on moving when the bus pulls up so they are all thrown to the front; on the other hand, when the bus starts, their inertia tends to keep them stationary so they are thrown in the other direction.

A common experience for children is the inertia of

water when they do a 'belly flop' at the swimming baths. They may also see a circus rider jump from a horse's back through a hoop and be interested to realise that she simply jumps vertically upwards. Inertia keeps her moving horizontally with the same speed as the horse underneath. The danger of throwing rubbish from a moving car or train is a relevant topic.

Tricks involving inertia

The following simple experiments are worth thinking about:

1

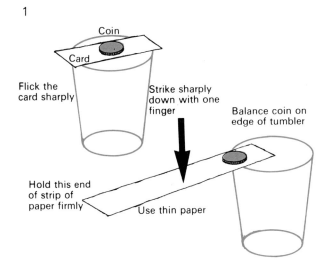

2. Make small holes in two table tennis balls.

Fill one with water, the other with a strong gelatine solution (table jelly will do) so that it sets hard.

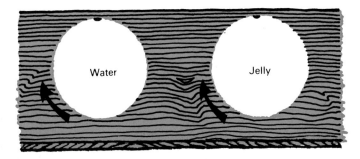

Seal up the holes.

Both balls should now be about the same weight. Spin each in turn on a smooth surface. Stop the ball momentarily with your fingers and immediately let go again. How do you explain what happens?

You have two eggs, one hard-boiled and the other raw. How can you quickly tell which is which?

3. Knock the bottom draught or coin from a pile by striking sharply with a ruler.

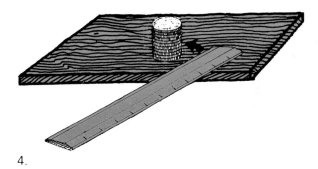

4.

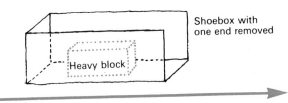

Move this way and stop rapidly

No doubt discussion of the use of seat belts will follow this experiment.

5. Someone will want to try the trick of moving the cloth from a table, leaving the crockery behind. See that both table and cloth are smooth ones, that the cloth is pulled rapidly and horizontally and that a good deal of practice is done first with objects on the cloth which are heavy but not breakable!

Will any of these inertia tricks work *slowly*? (Why they will not will probably not be clear at this point but we return to this problem later (page 34).)

How much force to start things moving?

Children can bring roller skates to try this. They can stand quite still on them while the pull needed just to get them started is measured. A large dial balance with a hook such as Salter's 5 kg is handy (Nuffield Item 85), but to construct a home-made force measurer for the job is much more fun, and one of those already made, (see page 15) if not already in the right range, can easily be converted to do the job.

An even simpler way is to push from behind with kitchen scales held horizontally.

What force is needed to move the heaviest member of the group? What force for the lightest? Is there a relationship between the push or pull needed and the weight of child?

Have we been fair in assuming all roller skates to be the same? Test the force needed to start individual roller skates moving. Are the differences big enough to matter? How much are your results affected by the surface you are working on?

Large trolleys

A very natural next move is to make pram-wheel trolleys. After racing these for general interest, a great many significant questions can be brought up. What have we got to do to be really fair about choosing the 'best' trolley? Does weight make any difference? Can you time first the heaviest child in the class and then the lightest on the same trolley over a fixed distance? But then can you be sure they were given the same push to start with?

This should involve a lot of thinking about giving an equal starting push. Do allow imagination free rein. Two easy ways are to start down slopes by releasing from the same height or to produce some kind of catapult, stretching it the same amount for each launching.

A good catapult may be made from several strands of 6-mm section rubber cord about 2 m long (for supplier see Appendix).

Having equal weights and an equal starting push, how do times compare over a fixed distance? Does the same trolley give the same result for each test? Do different people measure time differently? Should we take an average result?

Home-made timers

Most schools will have stop-watches or stop-clocks for the timing but it is a good challenge for a group to construct their own timer, in this case one which measures quite small intervals. One is constantly surprised at children's ingenuity and mechanical ability.

The most usual timers produced are basically some-thing which vibrates evenly, usually a pendulum of some kind.

Could you make a timer with a bouncing ball?

At first it is perfectly sound to time in ticks, swings or bounces but as soon as several people are timing the same trolley-run with different inventions the need for a standard unit is obvious. The timers may now be tuned

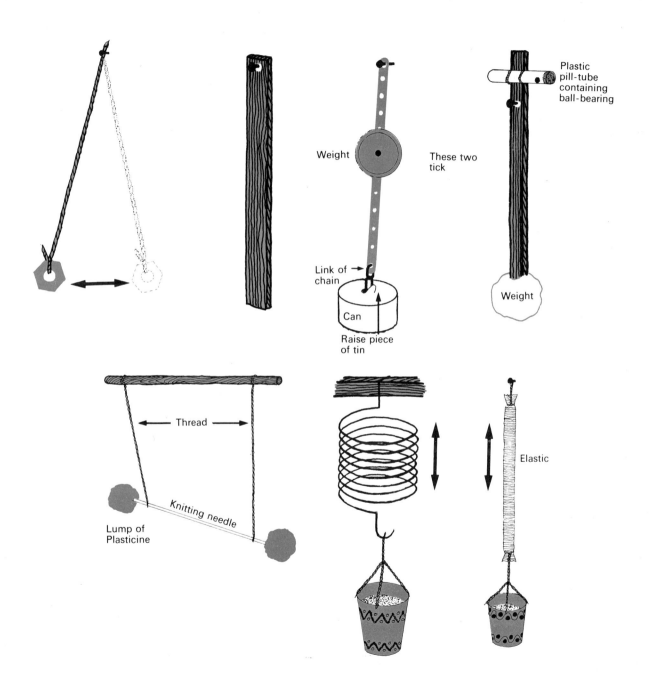

Weight

These two tick

Plastic pill-tube containing ball-bearing

Link of chain

Can

Raise piece of tin

Weight

Thread

Knitting needle

Lump of Plasticine

Elastic

21

to half-seconds, quarter-seconds, etc, by altering lengths and comparing with a clock or metronome. Alternatively they may simply be timed with a stop-watch, and a conversion factor of x swings per second noted.

Other timers are shown:

1. Drip-timer.

Either fill the original hole with Plasticine and make a fine hole in this with a needle or use a glycerine/water mixture instead of water, when the original hole can often be kept (see note in Appendix).

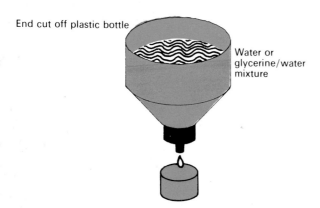

End cut off plastic bottle

Water or glycerine/water mixture

2. Rolling ball timer.

Adjust the height to adjust the interval timed.

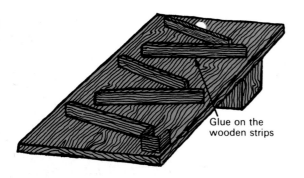

Glue on the wooden strips

3. Flasher-timer.

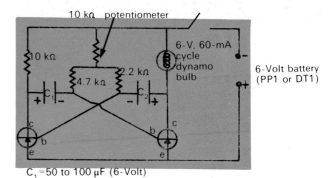

10 kΩ potentiometer

10 kΩ

2.2 kΩ

4.7 kΩ

6-V, 60-mA cycle dynamo bulb

6-Volt battery (PP1 or DT1)

C_1 C_2

C_1 = 50 to 100 μF (6-Volt)

C_2 = 5 μF (6-Volt)

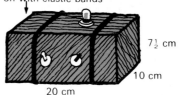

Transistors OC81, GET114 or equivalent:-

GET114   OC81

Wooden box with loose lid held on with elastic bands

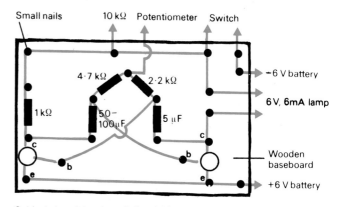

7½ cm

10 cm

20 cm

Small nails   10 kΩ Potentiometer Switch

4·7 kΩ   2·2 kΩ

1 kΩ

50–100 μF

5 μF

−6 V battery

6 V, 6mA lamp

Wooden baseboard

+6 V battery

Solder in transistors last of all and take care not to get them hot

It is often useful to be able to time by the ticks of a metronome (see Appendix on apparatus).

Measuring speeds

At this stage children will most likely take for granted that speed equals distance/time, so as they have now made timers they can have a good deal of experience measuring speeds of doing things, for example walking down corridors, running races and running the trolleys over different courses.

Another interesting occupation is to find the speed of traffic. The distance between two landmarks along a road is measured in metres and then the various traffic may be timed. Metres per second can be converted to kilometres per hour. What percentage of the traffic keeps to the speed limit?

A speedometer shows the speed at a particular moment

Children may now see, especially if the speed of a trolley over a long and perhaps hilly course is measured, that we have been measuring *average* speed but that there is another thing, instantaneous speed. This is the speed which is shown at any moment on the speedo-meter of a car. We could work it out if it were possible to measure the distance travelled for very small intervals of time.

This can be done by fixing a drip-timer to a trolley. Working on a playground, the drips are better seen if the water is brightly coloured with a dye. Where the

drips are further apart the trolley is going faster. If the drips have been timed, the speed of the trolley between any two of them can be calculated.

Sliding blocks

Several blocks of wood may be cut like the one shown. Each should be made to have the same weight; the size shown is just a suggestion.

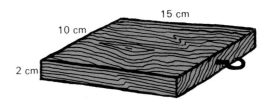

One block may be placed on a clean table or a piece of hardboard. How big a force is needed to start it moving? A selection of the force-measurers already devised (page 15) may be used to push or pull.

One school made a useful force-measurer for this experiment from a thin length of rubber from a rubber band, running through a plastic drinking straw with marks along its length.

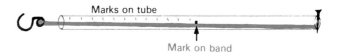

Marks on tube

Mark on band

A more rigid plastics or glass tube is better than a drinking straw.

Another design of force-measurer suitable for these experiments is shown in the following drawing. The elastic cord is an item from the Nuffield O-level apparatus (see Appendix). It has a ring already fixed at each end.

Hook

String

Elastic cord

Nail

Long piece of wood

Next try with two blocks one on top of the other, then with three and so on. Show the results on a graph. This is not an experiment for which anyone is likely to get precise and consistent measurements, but this does not mean that it is a 'bad' experiment which should not have been included. On the contrary, it is a useful illustration of a type of experimental situation which is very common. This question is taken up again in *Science, models and toys Stage 3* where the distance over which a toy mangonel can project cherry stones is recorded as a scatter graph.

Steady speed
Having recorded the force needed to start the block moving, keep an eye on the force-measurer as you move it along at a steady speed. (One can judge steady speed' reasonably well.) Is the force now greater than starting, or less, or the same, or zero? Try with different weights on the block.

Friction
What difference does it make to our experiments with the blocks to have them sliding on different surfaces? Try as many different surfaces as you can, for example the rough side of hardboard, different metals, different woods, foam rubber, glass, plastic, emery paper, leather, carpet. What effect do you get with different surfaces glued on to the bottom of the blocks as well?

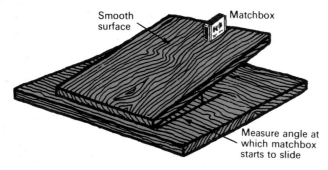

Smooth surface

Matchbox

Measure angle at which matchbox starts to slide

Will a matchbox slide better on a smooth side or on the sand-paper side? How are you going to try it?

Children should be allowed sufficient time to devise experimental methods in their own way and teachers should resist setting out a particular method at the

beginning and so lose all the valuable thinking which is the main reason for the activity.

Perhaps the simplest arrangement which a teacher would have in mind as the end of the experiment planning would be as shown in the diagram.

Does the grade of sand-paper matter?

If a set of similar blocks is made with sand-paper in a range of grades glued to one side of them, they may be lined up at the top of the slope and picked out in order of beginning to slide. The results may be rather surprising.

What other variables ought we to investigate? How does the force required to start moving change when you change the area of contact of the block and the surface it is resting on. For example, try sliding a matchbox first on the broad smooth side and then on the narrow smooth side. Finally all results may be compared using different materials for the *slope*.

A block may be pulled along a flat surface with a large area or a small area in contact, as shown in the drawings on the opposite page.

Does the *shape* of the area of contact matter? Blocks of equal weight and area to the original ones but in a multitude of shapes should be cut. If the same thickness of timber is used, this is very easily done by cutting paper patterns to the size of the original rectangle. These may then be cut up into pieces which can be put together in different ways to make different shapes. If they are pasted on to the wood the new shape may be cut out with a fretsaw.

The weight may be adjusted by adding a bit of wood on top or digging a bit out. Many irregular areas may have to be measured here. It might be quite a challenge to children who may have learned area as 'length times breadth'!

What difference do wheels make?

The blocks may now be pulled along, rolling on round pencils or pieces of dowel. Then the experiments may be repeated with a set of blocks fitted with wheels. (All blocks plus wheels should be of equal mass.)

Is the force needed to start still proportional to the mass, even if the forces in general are much smaller? Do different surfaces make much difference now?

Try out the same experiment with roller skates. Do the ball-bearings on the skates give different results from the cruder bearings on the blocks? Experiment with different-sized wheels wheels with tyres and without, and caterpillar tracks.

Try the effect of different bearings (eg dowel rod or nails through holes in wood, Meccano axles) and try

Each trolley an equal mass

A modern car wheel

Peat cart wheel 1800 B.C.

the effect of lubricating the bearings with various lubricants such as water, various kinds of oil, soap, French chalk (talc) and graphite (from a soft pencil).

The history of the development of wheels and tyres is interesting, and a look at the botany, geography and properties of rubber would not be out of place.

A general discussion on friction in everyday life will bring in walking, skating, writing, striking matches and bowing a violin. Friction is universal and while it always resists movement, we couldn't move in any of our normal ways without it. We should have to use jet motors for starting, stopping and turning as the astronauts do.

Friction on the road

The illustration shows a page from the Highway Code. Is the stopping distance in direct proportion to the speed? Why does there have to be a 'thinking distance'? How long do they reckon it takes you to think? Is this the time *you* take? (See reaction time experiments in Unit *Time*.) What are the variables they have not been able to take into account to make this page? (For example, worn and badly adjusted brakes; worn tyres; different weights of vehicles; people's health, eyesight, drinking habits, emotional state; condition of road; the weather.)

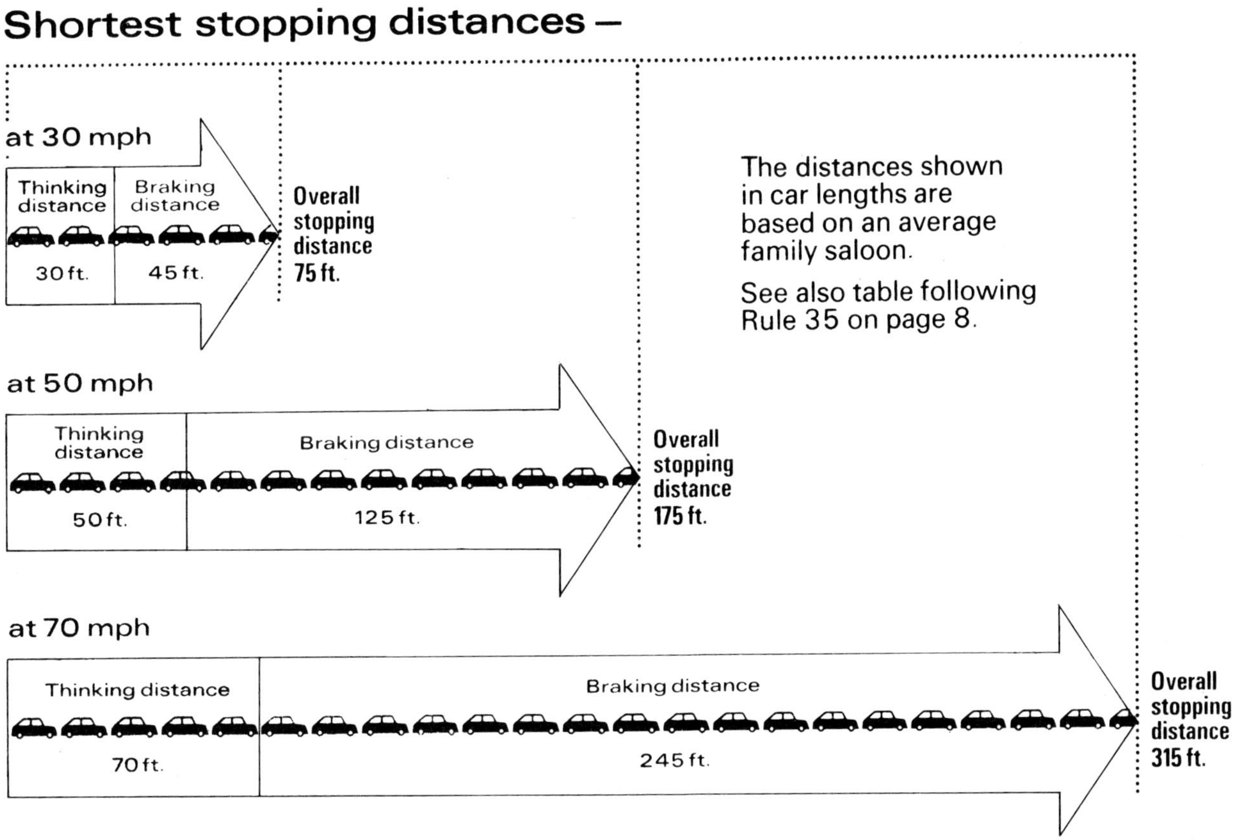

Shortest stopping distances —

at 30 mph

Thinking distance	Braking distance
30 ft.	45 ft.

Overall stopping distance **75 ft.**

at 50 mph

Thinking distance	Braking distance
50 ft.	125 ft.

Overall stopping distance **175 ft.**

at 70 mph

Thinking distance	Braking distance
70 ft.	245 ft.

Overall stopping distance **315 ft.**

The distances shown in car lengths are based on an average family saloon.

See also table following Rule 35 on page 8.

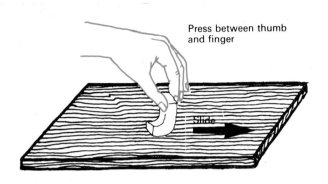

Press between thumb and finger

Slide

Push an india rubber along a piece of hardboard as shown. Next try the same thing but with some water on the board. Then try it with a layer of oil and with water on top of the oil.

Are the conditions of this experiment anything like those of a car tyre on a road? What do the results tell you about driving on the road in wet weather? This experiment is worth extending to try different 'road' surfaces and different tread patterns on the rubber, and to devise a way of *measuring* the effect rather than just feeling it.

Bicycles should be tested on the playground. First of all badly adjusted brakes and worn tyres could be looked for and stopping distances compared at roughly the same speed.

Stopping distances should be compared:

Skidding.

With brakes hard on but just *not* causing the wheels to skid.

The results are sometimes a surprise.

Frictional force is 'self adjusting'. It just balances the force applied up to a limit. Then sliding starts. The sliding friction is *less* than the maximum. Cars stop more quickly if we do not lock the wheels to make them skid and new brakes have been devised which release themselves slightly just before the point of locking. Skidding is prevented and the car pulls up in a shorter distance.

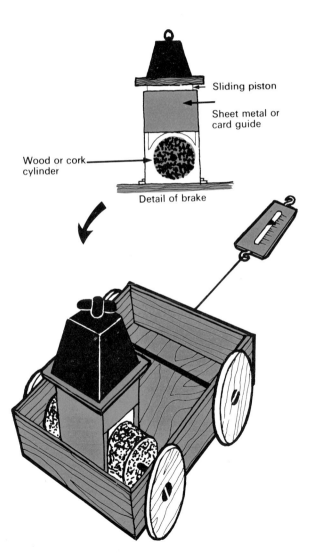

Sliding piston

Sheet metal or card guide

Wood or cork cylinder

Detail of brake

A trolley such as the one shown may be made and the pull to move it measured and recorded as the braking weight is increased up to the point where the wheels skid.

There could be a competition to invent the best brakes for the pram-wheel trolleys.

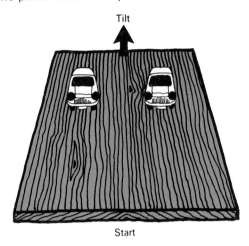

Tilt

Start

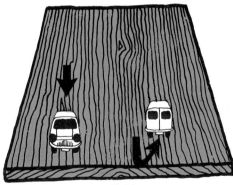

Finish

If one of two similar toy cars has its front wheels locked with a piece of Plasticine while the other has its back wheels locked, they may be placed together on a board which is slowly tilted.

What happens when they move down? (Remember that sliding friction is less than rolling friction.) Does this experiment suggest anything about the adjustment of car brakes?

Thinking a bit further

Experience so far has shown that a force is needed to start and stop things, and a smaller one to keep them going steadily. (Anyone knows that a car driver who accelerates and brakes furiously uses a lot more petrol than a 'steady type'.)

It might also have been noticed that as friction is reduced, the force to keep going becomes *much* smaller. What about the ideal case? Suppose there was no friction at all. This projection of ideas is typical of scientific thinking in general and children at Stage 3 are just becoming capable of it.

How near could we get to no friction?

Try giving an ice cube a push on a smooth hard plastic table-top. There is still some friction but not much. How far does the cube go if set off with a very small force from a pusher? Pull back the pusher a small distance and let it catapult forward to strike the cube.

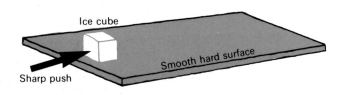

What force is enough to make the cube just reach the other side of the table?

Similar experiments should be tried with a block of wood on polystyrene beads. These beads should be on a large tray or in a channel as shown.

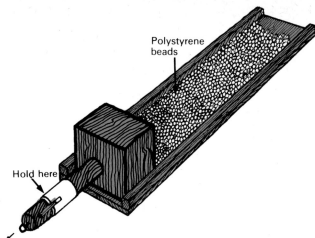

It is dangerous to spill polystyrene beads on the floor. One quickly learns the need for friction when walking, but falls can be nasty because they are unexpected. The beads are difficult to sweep up too. (A vacuum cleaner is a help.)

Why is it no use making really smooth roads to save petrol? It is not only the danger of skidding when braking—try running toys with motor-driven wheels on polystyrene beads.

With the Hot Wheels toy, a lubricant (polytetrafluorethylene) is provided to use on the bearings of the cars. Why is it not put on the roadway? Would it make any difference?

Acceleration

So we can think that if there was *no* friction, no force at all would be needed to keep things moving steadily. Forces would only be needed to change speed or, in other words, *accelerate* and *decelerate*. An accelerator on a car is familiar enough and these terms hardly need explaining as 'speed increasing' and 'speed decreasing'.

Children enjoy trying sprint starts to see who can accelerate the best. What is the best way to do it? Can you go on doing it? Does practice make an improvement? Is the ability to accelerate related to: length of legs, size of breath taken, sex, age?

Acceleration detectors

These may be made to use in cars, buses and trains.

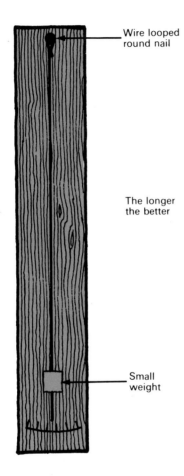

Wire looped round nail

The longer the better

Small weight

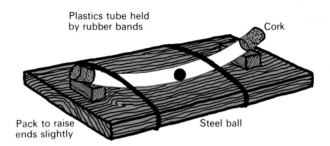

Plastics tube held by rubber bands

Cork

Pack to raise ends slightly

Steel ball

They are 'pointed' in the direction of motion. At steady speed the ball or pendulum bob rests centrally. Many children will need to be convinced of this by a practical test. An attempt might be made to mark the detectors with a scale to compare accelerations.

Obviously, all the instruments may also be used to measure decelerations.

One of the simplest ways of testing brakes which is used in practice is shown below. It consists simply of a set of tall blocks of wood set up on a horizontal surface. All the blocks have the same height but their square bases vary in size.

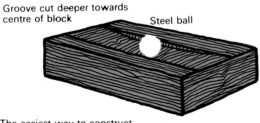

Groove cut deeper towards centre of block

Steel ball

The easiest way to construct this one is to bend a piece of thin plywood inside a shallow box

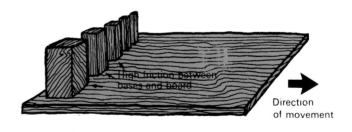

High friction between bases and board

Direction of movement

The degree of deceleration is shown by the number of blocks which fall over.

Acceleration of cars may be compared using lists from *The Motor* or *Autocar*. They are usually given like this:

Speed in mph	Time taken in seconds
0–30	3·3
0–40	5·0
0–50	6·9
0–60	9·1
0–70	12·9
0–80	17·2
0–90	23·7
0–100	35·3

It is interesting to draw speed/time graphs. The steeper the curve, the greater the acceleration.

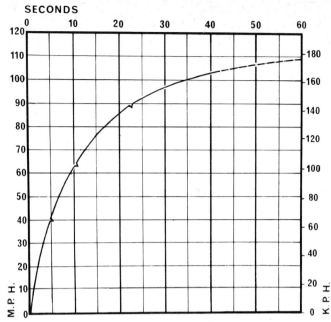

Ford Granada GXL and its acceleration data

Accelerating trolleys

What happens if you apply a steady force to a movable object when friction is as low as possible? A good way to begin to find out is to make a trolley like this one:

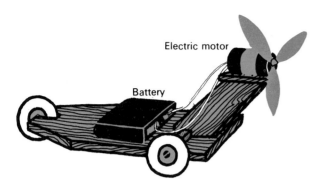

Electric motor

Battery

There is a more detailed diagram in the Appendix.

The battery is connected and the propeller drives the trolley across a floor or along a track. If the propeller is made to push, so that the single wheel is the front of the vehicle, slight knocks will usually cause no damage. If one of the acceleration detectors is mounted on the trolley it shows an acceleration all the time.

A metronome ticking seconds or half-seconds is needed. It can be home-made (see page 21) or bought (see Appendix). Teamwork is necessary now. The trolley, propeller spinning ready, is released on a count-down of 'ticks'. Children along the line of the run put a chalk mark at the place the front of the trolley reaches on each successive tick of the metronome. The chalk marks get further and further apart like this:

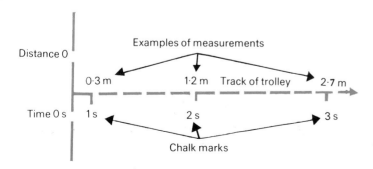

Of course, the run must be done several times and the chalk marks will form a cluster for each reading. A fair average position will have to be agreed.

It is clear that the trolley is accelerating. This may be as far as many children will want to go, perhaps making a graph of distance against time.

Others might go further. How much does the trolley accelerate? Is the acceleration steady? The average speeds between each chalk mark can be calculated (metres per second would be best). In the above example, the average speed between 0 and 1 second is 0·3 metres per second; between 0 and 2 seconds, 0·6 metres per second; between 0 and 3 seconds, 0·9 metres per second. The trolley started with no speed so at the chalk marks the speed must be two times the average.

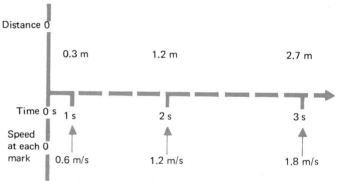

How much does the speed go up every second (acceleration)? Use your own figures from experiments. Do they suggest that a constant force produces a steady acceleration? Make a graph of speed against time. How could this help you to decide?

Fitted with a drip-timer (see page 82) the trolley may be made to time itself. It is probably best with this arrangement, to do the runs along a strip of paper so that the drips show up well. Lengths of wallpaper are very suitable.

Change the mass

Change the mass of the trolley by adding weights to it. How does this change the acceleration? Does there seem to be any rule about it? Check any ideas by taking further readings and making a graph of mass against acceleration.

Change the force

Up to this point a roughly constant force has been used. Can you now change the motor for a more powerful one and/or change the propeller blades (eg a three-bladed propeller in place of a two-bladed propeller). It is easiest to have a set of trolleys made. There are five sizes of motor easily available (see Appendix).

Do you get the same sort of results with a different force applied to the trolley?

What sort of results do you get using the trolley without wheels in a long 'channel' track spread with polystyrene beads? What happens to the acceleration if you add weights to double the mass of the trolley?

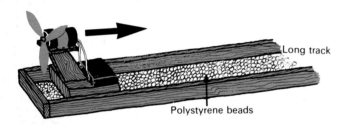

Long track

Polystyrene beads

Could you write down very simply what the relationship between force, mass and acceleration is likely to be if conditions were perfect? (In perfect conditions, of course, there would be no friction and no *air*—then our propeller system wouldn't work!)

We now have *another* way of measuring force (see page 15). A force can be measured by how much it accelerates a certain mass. This is how the *newton* is worked out as the unit of force. It is the force needed to cause 1 kg to increase its speed by 1 m/s, every second.

Summary

An unbalanced force accelerates or decelerates things. Balanced forces may be in an object which is still, like a bridge, or an object which is moving steadily with a constant velocity. Without any force on them at all, things stay still or keep moving at steady speeds in a straight line. (It *does* need a force to change direction or to go in a curve.)

There is no need to invent spirits to keep the universe moving. Once started, with no friction at all, it will go on for ever. Once put into orbit, artificial satellites keep moving steadily and space capsules, once launched, keep on without further forces being needed except to change direction or to slow up on return to earth.

Newton was the first to sort this out and this might be the right time to look at his story. He deserves a very great deal more than the usual vague anecdote about the apple and 'discovering gravity'. There is a helpful *Jackdaw* published with facsimiles of original material.

Inertia experiments again

Lift a brick slowly from the ground with a piece of thin twine.

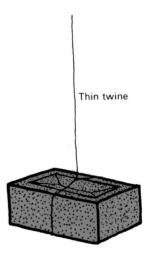

Thin twine

Then try to lift it quickly.

A small acceleration needs a small force and the twine is strong enough. A large acceleration needs a large force and the twine breaks.

Place an ice cube on a piece of glass. Move the glass slowly and the cube with it. Then try moving the glass more quickly. How do you explain this one?

On page 19 there were some tricks with inertia which could not be done *slowly*. When we tried to accelerate an object rapidly we needed to apply a large force to it, but in each arrangement we could pass on this force to the object only through two surfaces in frictional contact. The frictional force was not great enough and slipping occurred. For a slow acceleration, when only a small force is needed, the frictional force was great enough and the object moved.

Why does it hurt if you do a 'belly-flop' at the swimming baths? Your body makes its own volume of water accelerate rapidly and a large force is needed. If you take care to stretch out your arms and dive into the water as a long wedge shape, it takes longer to push the water aside. As it is not accelerating so rapidly less force is needed and so we feel a little less push back from the water.

Bumping into things

Usually bumping is something to be avoided especially with cars, ships and planes but sometimes it is useful, for example in all kinds of hammering processes and in railway shunting. It is also interesting to consider how very frequently bumping is used in our games

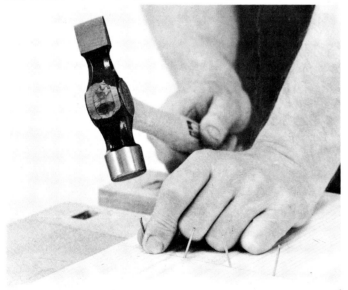

Some simple bumping experiments like the following are worth doing.

The effect of mass

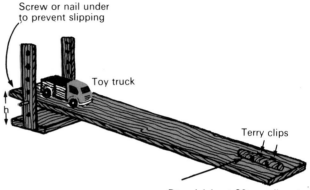

Screw or nail under to prevent slipping

Toy truck

Terry clips

Dowel (about 20 mm diameter)

Keeping the same slope on the track so that the velocity of impact is the same each time, load the truck with different numbers of heavy washers and measure the distance for which the dowel rod is knocked forward each time. Plot a graph.

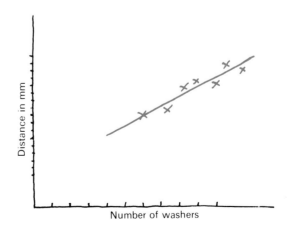

Distance in mm

Number of washers

The effect of velocity

Next, with a fixed load, vary the velocity of impact by tilting the slope. What effect does doubling the height of the slope have? (height=h in diagram). Try a graph of height of slope against distance rod is pushed forward.

If you crashed a car at 60 mph would you expect twice as bad a bump as at 30 mph?

Momentum

We need to be able to measure the *amount of motion* a thing has. A car at 100 mph will have ten times as much 'motion' as one at 10 mph, but obviously it isn't just the speed that matters, a seagull and a liner may be moving together at about 30 knots but they would take different 'amounts of stopping'!

So we take both mass (M) and velocity (V) into account and call M x V the *momentum*.

Even with good brakes which exert a large stopping force, large masses take a long time to stop because they have a large momentum. Collect examples (eg oil tankers, trains, aeroplanes). On the other hand there are objects which have a large momentum because of their large velocity even if their mass is small. Examples would be space capsules, meteorites, bullets.

An experiment on momentum

Pull the trolleys apart so that the elastic is stretched, and fix in this position with a length of cotton round nails as shown. The elastic will exert an equal force on each trolley.

How will you arrange the match-sticks to test if the speed of each trolley is the same? Do it.

Has each trolley the same momentum at any time?

Next load one of the trolleys to make its mass 2M. If the trolleys still have equal momentum when the cotton is burnt through, how might the speeds be different?

How do we set up the match-sticks to test our guess?

Can you test 3M against M and 3M against 2M?

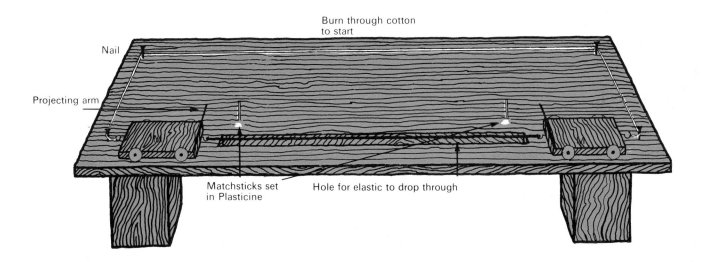

Burn through cotton to start

Nail

Projecting arm

Matchsticks set in Plasticine

Hole for elastic to drop through

(Note. Trolleys have equal mass, M)

Time taken to stop

Nothing can stop instantly. A car hitting a wall takes a small time to stop while the front is pushed in and the wall knocked over. Even in a small bump, which does no damage, a little time is taken, (for example while the bumper is compressed a little and springs back again). If you throw a ball of clay at a wall it might seem to take no time at all to stop but if you look at the shape of the clay afterwards you will realise that a short time was needed for a force to cause the change.

So for stopping things we can have a large stopping force for a short time, a small stopping force for a long time or some arrangement in between, the amount (force x time) depending how big the momentum of the thing was before stopping began.

Distance to stop

So you can see that a car travelling at 60 mph will take twice as long to stop as it would if travelling at 30 mph. (Assuming braking forces equal.) It has twice as much *momentum* and will take *four times* the distance to stop because not only will the time taken be twice as big, but the average speed over the stopping distance will also be twice as big (in this case 30 mph instead of 15 mph).

This was something suggested by the experiment on page 28. A bicycle can be skidded to a stop from various speeds and the distances measured. If the bicycle can be fitted with a speedometer it makes matters simpler.

Gravity: a force which acts on everything all the time

Gravity, probably approached from the point of view of space travel, would make a good alternative starting point for the work of this Unit. It is one of our very earliest experiences that everything falls to the ground. We enjoy the effect of gravity as we push toys from our pram, but find it a little more frustrating as we try to walk. Gravity isn't discovered; it is experienced! Our experience is that things fall to the ground. We explain it by saying there must be a force, and we call the force gravity. Newton's great imaginative step forward came when he realised that the apple pulled the earth as much as the earth pulled the apple and, in fact, when the apple fell, the earth moved a tiny distance towards the apple as well.

It is the force of gravity acting on masses which gives them weight and it is very convenient to compare masses on earth by weighing them. But this will not do if we get away from the earth's surface. When a space station is being made the girders will have no weight but it will take just as much force to move them as on earth because they still have the same mass. A mechanic will just as easily bruise his thumb with a weightless hammer and he will have to take care not to be crushed between two weightless (but massive) girders.

Dropping things from a height

Try dropping a large variety of objects, starting them off together a few at a time. Don't forget natural objects including leaves and fruits, winged and otherwise. One cannot get enough height in a classroom but there are many other possibilities such as galleries, balconies, stair-wells, upper windows and flat roofs. (Take proper precautions, of course, both at top and bottom.)

All kinds of unexpected things happen. Don't be rushed by the child who has *read* about Galileo into not allowing children to investigate for themselves. The importance of looking for oneself was what Galileo was trying to preach!

'Nor wrest I any Experiment to make it quadrare with any pre-conceived Notion.' Robert Hooke (1661).

Things will spin, travel at different speeds, move in odd directions and in general behave differently according to shape and size.

It would be worth having a competition to make the object which would fall most slowly or to make a package, no bigger than a shoebox, say, in which an egg could be soft-landed from the school roof on to a hard playground.

The various falling objects should be timed and many kinds of timers should be invented and used (see page 20). Remember Galileo had no watch. He had to use pulse rates and water dripping from a can, which he weighed (see Unit, *Time*).

Air resistance

It will be clear that the air has an effect on the way things fall.

1. Allow a sheet of paper to fall and then compare the effect when it is screwed up. *Why* does a sheet of paper always fall so that it offers maximum resistance to the air? Can you possibly make a sheet of paper fall 'edgeways on'?

Try increasing the thickness of the sheet (use cardboard and sheets of plywood). Is there a thickness where the effect stops? What happens if you alter the area of the sheet?

Try pushing or pulling sheets of material through water to see if you get the same effect (see 'Boats' in *Science from toys*).

2. Design and test model parachutes. Compare different cloths and plastics. Compare different sizes and the effect of different weights on the bottom.

Does a hole in the top make a difference?

Does the size of this hole matter?

Does it have a different effect in different materials?

3. How fast do balloons fall?

Do different sizes fall at different rates?

Try the rate of fall of different-sized bubbles. (Use a half and half mixture of Stergene and water.)

4. Make all kinds of model gliders, and compete for the longest period in the air. What is (*a*) the distance record, (*b*) the time of flight record, for a glider made from a post-card?

What are the records for a glider made from an expanded polystyrene ceiling tile? (Use a glue such as Copydex or Evo-stik woodworking adhesive.)

For a 'fair throw' children can devise a catapult. About the simplest design would be that shown in the drawing.

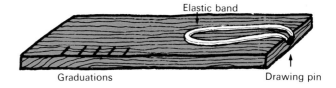

Elastic band

Graduations   Drawing pin

There could be an extensive 'side-line' on flight at this point and there would be no harm in that.

5. Can you invent an experiment to find how air resistance changes with speed ? For example, you might rig up a cardboard 'sail' on a trolley and try towing it with a force-measurer at different speeds to find the different pull needed. Does doubling the speed double the push of the air ?

What happens if you keep the speed the same (ie take the same time to pull the trolley along a fixed distance) but alter the area of the sail ? Does doubling the sail area double the push of the air ?

Does the shape of the sail matter ? Try different shapes with equal area. For example how do these three compare ?

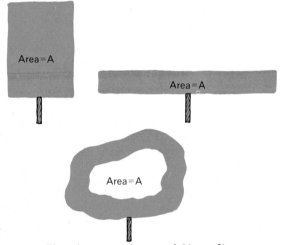

(How do you get the area of this one ?)

Some schools have found the above difficult to do with any satisfaction but have had success with the following:

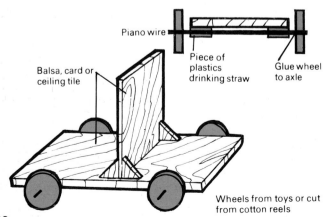

A small, lightweight trolley is made from balsa or card with a set of interchangeable sails of different areas and shapes. A hair drier or fan is used to blow on the sail (one of the trolleys described on page 82 acts as a fan when held in the hand). The time to travel a certain distance can be related on a graph to the area of the sail.

6. With the apparatus shown in the drawing below, a set of cards having different areas may be made to fit the slit in the reel (a saw-cut about 3 mm deep).

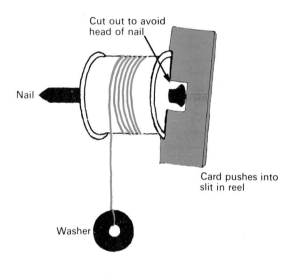

The washer accelerates at first but soon starts falling at a steady speed. This happens when the turning effect of its weight just balances that of air resistance on the card plus friction on the nail. (*Both* these increase as the cards get bigger.)

Measure the time for the washer to fall the full length of the string, first without any card in the slot and then for different cards. Make a graph of time against area of card. Can you guess from the graph what area of card will not turn at all ? Try it out. (But if the card isn't turning at all, there can't be *any* air resistance. What is the force which is stopping it ?) How much do you have to cut off to get it turning ?

Viscosity of liquids

The frictional effect is shown by liquids even more than by air. It is called *viscosity*. There is a good deal of interesting experimental work.

1. Comparing different liquids.

The viscosity of different liquids may be compared by finding the time taken for a small (eg 5 mm) ball-bearing to fall through each of them in, say, an Alka-Seltzer tube.

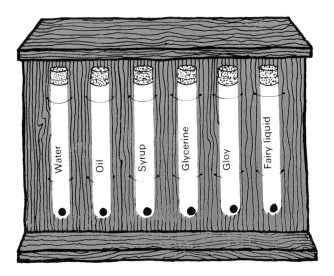

Try many liquids including water, golden syrup, glycerine, liquid detergents, Gloy and several grades of oil. Tubes used should not be less than 1 cm in diameter and the longer the better. They could be of wide plastic tubing corked at each end, and if a set is mounted on a board, they may be inverted together to start a race. If test-tubes are used, don't forget that a ball-bearing dropped in without any liquid present will knock the end off! A small pad glued to the bottom would help.

2. Does the width of tube make any difference? With the same size ball in each case, use oil or glycerine in different diameter tubes to find out.

Several tubes could be mounted on a board together as shown above. Experiments should also be made with different sizes of ball in the same tube. One group made a timer from a half-metre length of 1-cm diameter tube full of water and a ball which almost, but not quite, fitted it.

3. Does temperature make a difference?

Compare results after liquids have been standing:

a. Over a radiator.

b. In a refrigerator.

Does a change of temperature make a bigger difference to some liquids than to others?

4. Find the difference between the viscosity of different grades of motor oil and then compare different *makes* of motor oil of the same grade. Do you think some of the advertising is honest (as far as viscosity is concerned)?

Another good way to compare viscosities is to use plastic syringes (see Appendix note on apparatus). The size is not very important but 5 ml is convenient.

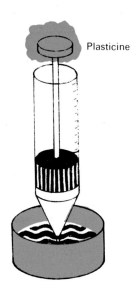

Plasticine

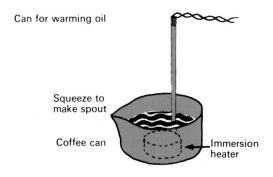

Plastics bottle with base cut off

Can lid with large hole

Base of plastics bottle

The liquid is drawn into the syringe and a standard pressure put on the plunger (eg by a known mass of Plasticine).

The time to squeeze out a measured quantity of liquid (eg 5 ml) is taken.

How do results compare with those from the experiments with the falling ball-bearing ?

5. How the viscosity of motor oil changes with temperature.

The oil is heated in a can by any convenient means, eg a hot-plate or small immersion heater (see Appendix).

Take the time for the oil to run out between two marks on the inverted bottle, and make a graph of the time for

Can for warming oil

Squeeze to make spout

Coffee can

Immersion heater

different temperatures. One can simulate winter starting conditions by beginning with oil which has been kept in a refrigerator.

Gear oil gives marked differences and other liquids, like concentrated detergent and golden syrup, are worth trying.

Terminal velocity

An interesting point to discuss shows up quite clearly in the experiments where a ball falls through liquids. Very soon it stops accelerating and moves at a steady speed. This is called its *terminal velocity*. Objects falling through the air reach a terminal velocity too, but not until they have travelled much further than in liquids and the velocity itself is much greater.

Thus a man jumping from a plane and delaying the opening of his parachute accelerates for a time but then reaches a steady speed of about 120 to 150 mph [190-240 km/h] because of air 'viscosity'.

Luckily for us there is a maximum speed for raindrops and hailstones, however far they have fallen.

Furry animals have quite a low terminal velocity and often fall from heights with comparative safety.

The flow of liquids, and streamlining for movement in water would be excellent side-line topics here (see *Holes, gaps and cavities* and *Science from toys*).

Thinking a bit further about gravity

Can we simplify our ideas about falling objects? Suppose there wasn't any air: surely there would be *no* friction then. What would happen? (For a long time it was believed that a vacuum was an impossibility so thinking like this seemed to be nonsense!)

1. We could try dropping objects for which the air resistance makes little difference. They would have to be fairly heavy, smooth and rounded. Try it with stones, cricket and golf balls, marbles and ball-bearings. The result can still be a surprise as it was in Galileo's time. If they fall on to a metal sheet one can hear how exactly they fall together.

2. Can you get a rough idea of the acceleration due to gravity? (This is usually called 'g'.)

As an example, suppose a stone is dropped seven metres and, as near as can be measured, the time taken is 1·2 seconds. Its average velocity will be:

$$\frac{700}{1\cdot2} \text{ cm per second} = 600 \text{ cm per second (approximately).}$$

[Centimetres per second is usually abbreviated to cm/s.]

As it started with no velocity, its final velocity will be twice this average.

Final velocity = 1200 cm/s.

So its acceleration $= \dfrac{1200}{1\cdot2} = 1000$ cm per second per second approximately.

[Usually written 1000 cm/s².]

After a lot of tries, the chief experience will be of how very difficult it is to do the timing and what a great variation there is in the results, because a small error in timing makes a lot of difference to the answer. This experience is well worth having!

3. Can we do better?

We might increase the height from which the stone is dropped, but for many this is not easy and the operator at the top becomes a long way from the observer at the bottom. In this case it is best to use two stop-watches. These are synchronised to start with and both are going. One is stopped by the operator at the top when the ball is released and the other is stopped by the observer at the bottom as the ball hits the ground.

It is much easier to use a slope. This was Galileo's idea for 'diluting the force'.

Experiments with a slope

Friction is a nuisance, but if we tilt the slope to start with so that the object on it is on the point of running down (but not quite) we could reckon to have compensated for friction.

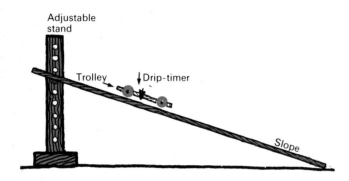

Adjustable stand

Trolley

Drip-timer

Slope

Tilt the slope a little more. Can you show that the trolley accelerates down the slope? (See Appendix, p. 82, for design of small drip-timer.)

Can you show that as the slope is increased the acceleration increases?

Can you show that changing the mass of the trolley doesn't make any difference? (Gravity simply pulls bigger masses harder in proportion to their masses.)

Can you show that the velocity of the trolley at any point is proportional to the time? (ie if we double the time the velocity doubles.)

Stage 3 children will possibly have reached the stage in mathematics where they know that a straight-line graph shows two quantities to be proportional, and this concept can be used.

In addition try graphs of distance travelled by the trolley against time taken and also suggest that distance against (time)^2 is tried.

It will be seen by most children that to find the value of g one would have to have the slope vertical. Some will agree that if you get the acceleration a on a slope like this:

h

l

Acceleration=a

then g will be: $a \times \dfrac{l}{h}$ if the slope is smooth.

A rough value may be calculated to compare with that obtained before.

Throwing things

A force-measurer or a simple piece of elastic may be used to project a steel ball or a marble horizontally from a table with different forces.

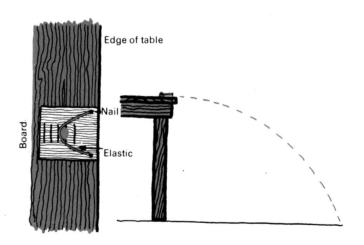

Edge of table

Nail

Board

Elastic

The path of the projected ball can be noted and the distance from the table at which it strikes the ground may be measured.

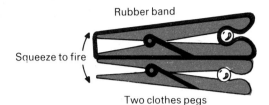

Rubber band

Squeeze to fire

Two clothes pegs

Path of a projectile

The path which a projected object takes through the air can be plotted using apparatus similar to that shown in the drawing.

A ball is projected from part *A*, using the same stretch of elastic each time. The board *B* is arranged at different distances (*x*) from the end of the slope. Each time the ball is projected it will make a mark on the paper clipped to *B* and the height of this (*y*) can be measured. A graph of *y* against *x* will show the shape of the path of the ball.

Next different angles of projection may be tried and the shapes of the paths compared. Which angle of throw *does* send the ball the greatest distance?

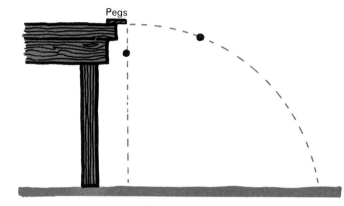

Pegs

With the simple apparatus shown (see *School Science Review*, vol. 51, no. 175, page 409) it is easy to compare a ball shot horizontally with one allowed to fall vertically, starting at the same time.

How far can you throw a tennis ball? What is the best angle to throw in order for it to go the greatest distance?

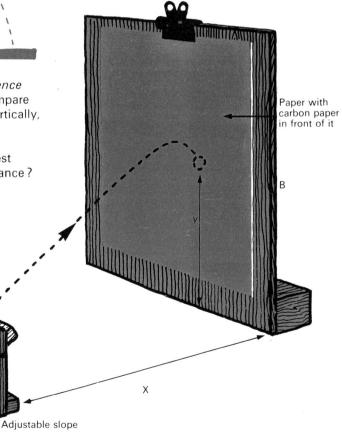

Paper with carbon paper in front of it

B

y

Groove

Elastic

X

Adjustable slope

A

Several trial schools improved on the simple projection system of the apparatus in many ways. The following is worth recording:

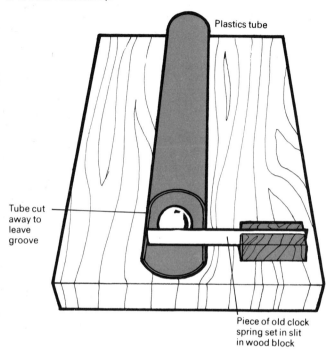

Plastics tube

Tube cut away to leave groove

Piece of old clock spring set in slit in wood block

For safety considerations thought should be given to the dimensions of the apparatus, especially the strength of elastic and of springs, and also to the nature of the supervision required for the particular group using it.

Orbiting the earth

The harder you throw a ball, the further away it would fall until, if only you could throw hard enough, it would travel right round the earth and go into orbit!

You would need to throw it at five or six miles per second (8–9 km/s) and that would need a powerful rocket. Near the earth the air would rapidly slow up the ball and cause it to fall, but if it had been sent up outside the earth's atmosphere it would travel on for ever.

At this point, time should be taken to collect information about rockets, satellites and space journeys. Development of our ability to throw things has proceeded very rapidly indeed since 1960!

Rotating things

Can you collect lists, pictures and examples of things which spin? It will include wheels, tops, record players and spin driers no doubt, but whirligig beetles and winged seeds should be investigated as well.

We ourselves are rotating with the earth at a rapid rate, the earth orbits the sun (which itself is spinning) and the sun moves round our galaxy. Some departure into simple astronomy would be very suitable here.

1. Use one of your force-measurers to find the force needed to close a door at different distances from the hinges or to turn a nut at different distances along a spanner.

For each case make a table:

F	r	F x r

What do you notice?

F × r is called the *torque*.

Find other torques, eg to turn different doors, a bicycle wheel, a car wheel, bicycle pedals, the key of a clockwork toy.

Can you find the torque needed to loosen the nuts holding a car wheel? Find the *correct* torque and tighten them up properly.

What is meant by a car report in *The Motor* which says maximum torque, 70 ft lb is developed at 2400 rev/min?

One day the motor magazines may give torques in Newton-metres (N-m), but not yet.

2. What do the figures 78, 45, 33, 16 on a record player mean? Can you check a record player to see whether it is going at the right speeds?

3. A simple 'spin drier' can be made from an empty squeezy bottle.

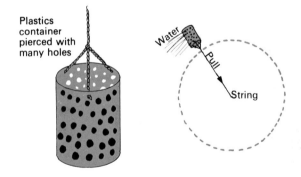

Plastics container pierced with many holes

Put the wet 'washing' in the container and swing it in a circle round your head on the end of a string. A pull is needed on the string to keep the bottle moving in a circle. The water drops are only very loosely 'tied'. In what direction do they move?

Weigh the container and contents before and after spinning, then dry the 'washing' thoroughly and weigh again to find what percentage of the water you got out by spinning.

Find the effect of using different lengths of string and different containers. What is the most efficient model you can make?

Rotating things: Cleaning turbine blades at Thorpe Marsh Power Station *(left)*, and a still from the film *Modern Times (right)*.

4. A toy reaction turbine may be constructed as shown:

Make four or more holes near the bottom of a tall can by knocking in a small nail. Turn each nail before pulling it out so that when water is put in the can the shape of the holes makes it spurt out in a tangential direction (see the drawings).

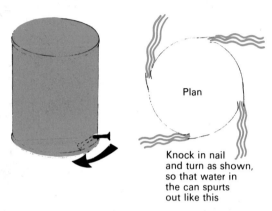

Plan

Knock in nail and turn as shown, so that water in the can spurts out like this

Either suspend the can or support it on ball-bearings on a slightly larger lid.

Working over a bowl or sink, fill the can with water.

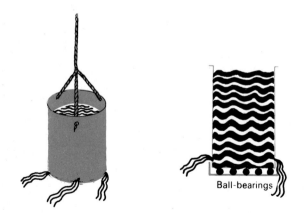

Ball-bearings

Which way does it turn?

What are the forces which make it turn?

What energy changes take place?

5. Some schools have deep stair-wells or similar places where it is possible to suspend a very long pendulum. It is then worth making a 'Foucault's pendulum' and attempting to show the spin of the earth.

The suspension must be free to turn in any direction and the very simplest design is shown in the drawing.

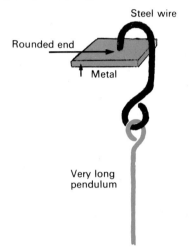

Steel wire

Rounded end

Metal

Very long pendulum

The pendulum bob, which should be as heavy as possible, is released to swing along a straight line marked on the floor.

The direction of the line of swing appears to change as time goes on although really it is fixed in space and the effect is due to the turn of the earth.

Motions which keep on repeating themselves

Sometimes forces cause repeating movements to take place. Many examples from everyday life may be collected, both from the many moving parts of machinery such as pistons, windscreen wipers and balance wheels in watches and clocks, and also from natural movements like the swaying of the bough of a tree, the flapping of birds' and insects' wings and the bobbing up and down of a small boat on the waves of the sea.

Many interesting investigations may be made:

Pendulums
Already mentioned on page 20 as 'timers'.

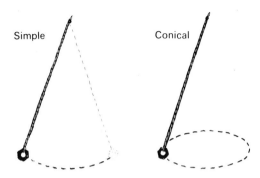

Simple   Conical

How does the time of swing change when you change the length of the string, the mass on the end and the size of swing?

Look at the complicated movements of pendulums in skittle games and also in the pattern making activities outlined in the Unit *Time*.

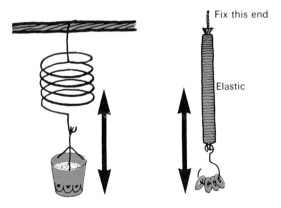

Fix this end

Elastic

It is interesting to compare the motions shown in the above drawing with those of pendulums. In this case, change the mass on the end, the length of the elastic (or the number of turns of the spring), the cross-section of the elastic, the diameter of the spring or the material from which it is made, to see what difference these make. Your own springs may be wound from different kinds of wire.

For any particular spring or elastic make a graph of the time for twenty bounces against the mass on the end for a range of masses. Can you use this for weighing objects?

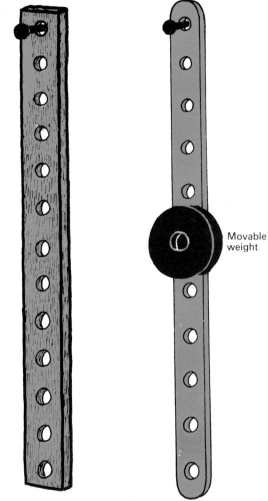

Movable weight

Bar pendulums (Meccano strips, lengths of pegboard, etc)

How does the time of swing of a bar pendulum differ from that of a string pendulum of the same length?

How does it change if you fix a weight on the bar in different positions?

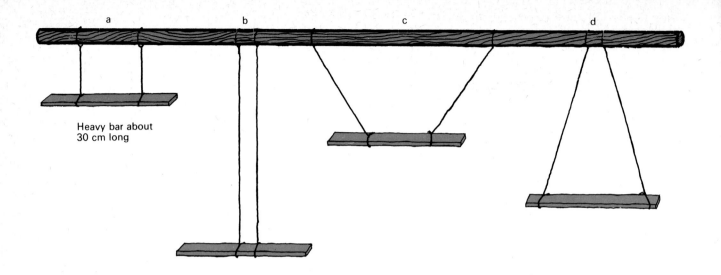

Heavy bar about
30 cm long

What happens if a pendulum has two strings instead of one ? What happens if you change the length of the strings, their distance apart, or have them at different distances apart at each end ?

What happens if you change the heavy bar shown in the drawing for a light knitting needle weighted with balls of Plasticine at the ends ? Try the balls in different positions along the needle. Are you changing the weight ? Does the time of swing change ?

Investigate a ball-bearing rolling on curtain track.

Are these like pendulums ?

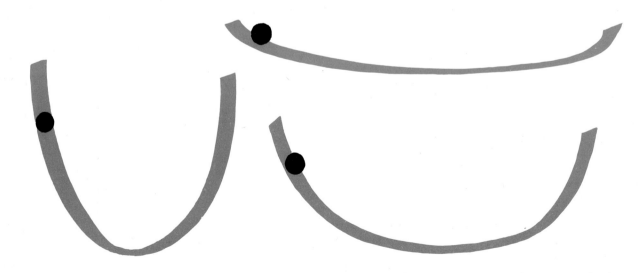

Swish curtain rail has a convenient groove into which one may slide a screwhead:

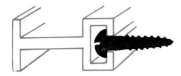

A number of these screws may then be pushed into a vertical piece of peg-board to bend the track to the shape required.

Try water in a U-tube. Suck a little up one arm and then let it fall.

How do the dimensions of the tube alter what happens?

Does another liquid, eg oil, behave differently?

Suspend a heavy object on a long piece of fairly fine wire. Twist and release it.

What difference does weight on the end, length, diameter and kind of wire make? Try string and nylon fishing line.

Can you find a clock which works like this?

Try the effect of using a weight made as shown. Move the blobs to different distances from the suspending wire.

Look at the movement of the balance wheel of a watch or clock.

Can you make a model of this movement using a larger spring, eg from a broken toy?

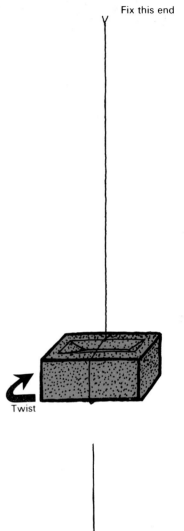

Fix this end

Twist

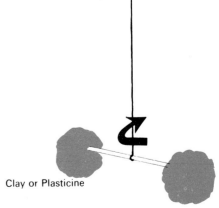

Clay or Plasticine

Vibrations

Look at the vibrations of a hacksaw blade arranged like this:

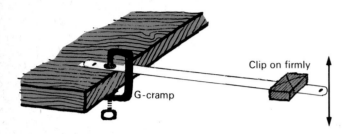

Clip on firmly

G-cramp

Try fixing different masses on the end. Time twenty vibrations of the blade alone. Clip a weight on the end and time again, and continue with increasing weights. Plot a graph of time for twenty vibrations against weight on the end.

Can you now use the blade as a weighing machine? Try strips of different materials. Try different lengths of strip. When do the vibrations make sounds?

Try making sounds by plucking strings and wires.

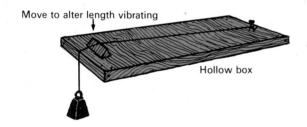

Move to alter length vibrating

Hollow box

What difference does the length of string make?

What difference does the tension of the string make?

What difference does the kind of string make?

Try as many different kinds and diameters of strings and wires as you can.

Find out what is vibrating to make the sound in a variety of musical instruments. (The work here could branch off into a study of sound.)

A trolley may be arranged in either of the ways shown below. The table and bearings should be as smooth as possible. Springs from the Nuffield Elasticity Kit may be used (see Appendix), model aeroplane elastic, or elastic bands looped together. Start with both sides under slight tension. Move the trolley to one side and let go.

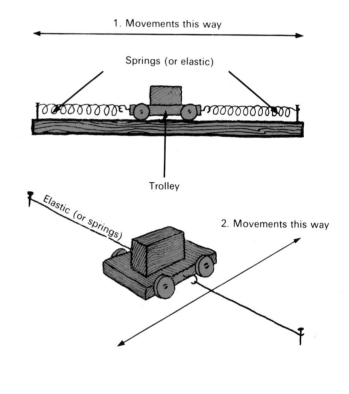

1. Movements this way

Springs (or elastic)

Trolley

Elastic (or springs)

2. Movements this way

Take the time for several oscillations and get the average time for one. This is called the *period*, ie the time taken starting from a certain position, to come back to the same place again. Repeat the timing with different loads on the trolley and make a graph of period against mass.

Use the graph for weighing things. How accurate is this 'weighing machine'?

Mostly about tensions

The aim of this part of the Unit is to suggest possible lines of activity for a group of children who have been looking at materials and structures as is suggested in the Unit *Structures and forces Stages 1 & 2*, but who are progressing in ability further than this.

Having looked with interest at bridges, cranes or spiders' webs they might be ready to think about forces and their action on materials in a more general way. But they will still need to spend a great deal of time on practical experiences: the whole idea of what follows is to help these developing children *towards* ideas of tensile strength, Hooke's law and the elastic properties of materials, and the nature of liquid surfaces. Mathematical generalisations may come later on but not before the children have had sufficient foundation in experience to understand them.

Tensions and compressions

'Tension' is an everyday word. Something undergoing tension has forces acting on it which are trying to stretch it. We even use the word figuratively to describe what our nerves feel like at times. We take an aspirin 'to relieve the tension'.

This beam is in tension

It is interesting that when we pull outwards on something there is a pull back inside the material which is *equal* to our outward pull as long as the material doesn't stretch. If there were not this resistance to tension, the material would give way.

If we do things the opposite way round, we have a *compression*.

This beam is in compression

It would be worth while thinking where the tensions and compressions are in bridges, buildings, cranes and other structures such as those we looked at in Stages 1 and 2 of the Unit. Two examples are shown in the drawings:

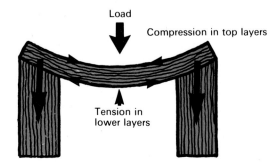

Beam bridge under load

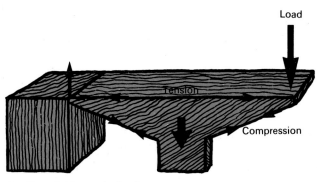

Cantilever bridge under load

It might be interesting to look at a flow chart showing work which developed from thinking how the forces go when an umbrella is put up:

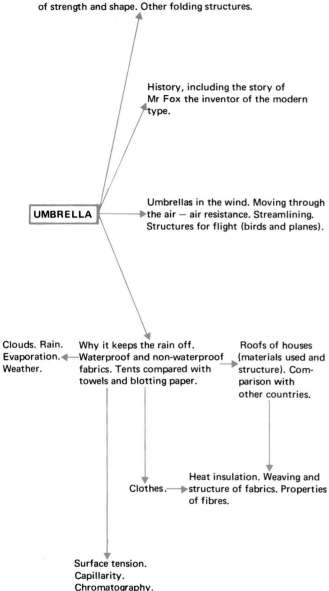

Structures: How the forces go when you put it up. Different kinds of umbrellas. Balancing forces keep it in tension. Shape of ribs — relation of strength and shape. Other folding structures.

History, including the story of Mr Fox the inventor of the modern type.

UMBRELLA

Umbrellas in the wind. Moving through the air — air resistance. Streamlining. Structures for flight (birds and planes).

Clouds. Rain. Evaporation. Weather.

Why it keeps the rain off. Waterproof and non-waterproof fabrics. Tents compared with towels and blotting paper.

Roofs of houses (materials used and structure). Comparison with other countries.

Clothes.

Heat insulation. Weaving and structure of fabrics. Properties of fibres.

Surface tension. Capillarity. Chromatography.

There is pleasure and real learning involved in such an outward-looking approach. When children have reached Stage 3 they still need sometimes to learn from topics in this way.

Strength and shape

How materials behave when forces are put on them depends not only on what the material is and how big the force which is acting, but also on the particular size and shape of the piece being tested. (See *Structures and forces Stages 1 & 2*, page 61, and 'Inventing force-measurers', page 15 of this Unit).

One could continue earlier interests by having a competition to produce the strongest girder 1 m long. Either one could restrict the materials to be used. eg to balsa wood or card, or give a maximum weight for the finished beam.

A group could investigate the behaviour of beams with the cross-sections shown in the drawings. If wood is used, see that the grain is similar in each test piece.

B, C, D and E all have the same area of cross-section but B is roughly twice C four times and D sixteen times as strong as A. E will be difficult to test without buckling.

Cross-sections of beams (dimensions in centimetres)

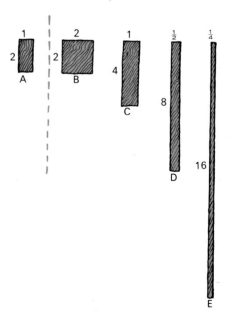

In steel girders, most of the steel is usually put into the flanges to resist bending forces while seeing that the web is sufficiently strong to prevent shear.

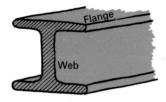

What weight is needed to crush a drawing-paper tetrahedron with 5-cm sides? How does the result compare with a model with 2·5-cm sides or 10-cm sides? How does the strength of a tetrahedron compare with other regular shapes made from drawing paper and having the same length of side (eg cubes)?

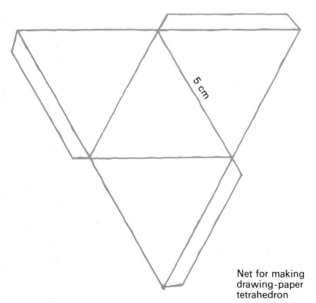

Net for making drawing-paper tetrahedron

An elastic shape
A metal wire, tested by pulling lengthwise with our hands, might be classed as rigid. It certainly doesn't seem very elastic. But what happens if we wind it round a cylinder and make it into a spiral shape (a helix)?

Try doing this with wire of as many different metals and alloys as you can obtain and also use other filaments such as nylon if this is possible. Range the materials in order from good spring makers to bad spring makers.

What difference does the thickness of the wire make?

What difference does the diameter of the spiral coil make?

Can you invent better ways of testing 'springiness' than pressing or pulling with your fingers?

Spring experiments
The next section suggests some experiments which might follow as a possible extension. Convenient spiral springs are made from a Slinky toy which is cut up into 5-, 10-, 15-, 20- and 25-turn coils. The material is brittle and snaps easily using a pair of pliers. Bends should be made gently using a thumb and forefinger.

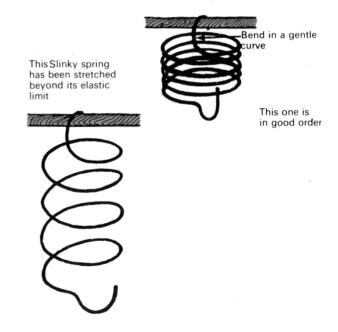

This Slinky spring has been stretched beyond its elastic limit

Bend in a gentle curve

This one is in good order

The only trouble about Slinky springs is that they are easily stretched beyond their elastic limit so that they remain with the coils 'open'. Care will be needed to prevent this happening too frequently.

The springs fit firmly into a saw-cut in a strip of wood.

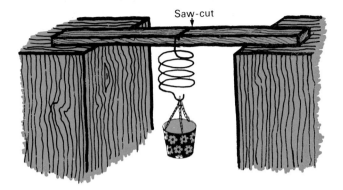

Saw-cut

1. Load different springs by dropping three marbles in the container.

How many *kinds* of motion does a spring have when you do this?

Which of the springs (with different numbers of turns) stretches most with three marbles?

2 Take one spring and measure the extension each time that a marble is added to the container (not more than five marbles). Make a graph of number of marbles against extension.

Do this again using a spring with twice as many turns.

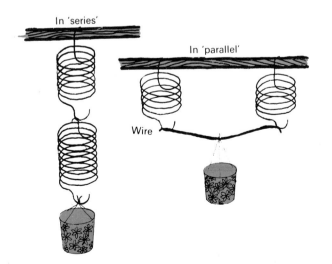

In 'series'

In 'parallel'

Wire

Draw the graph using the same axes as the first one. Are the stretch graphs similar? How are they different? Try a spring with a different number of turns and see where the graph fits in this time.

Do you get the same sort of graph if you use a rubber band instead of a spring? Try several sizes of rubber band. Would you choose a spring or rubber for making a weighing machine?

3. Compare the stretch graph for one 20-turn spring with that for two 10-turn springs (*a*) in series, (*b*) in parallel (see lower diagram).

4. Will a 5-marble load on a spring bounce more rapidly or more slowly than a 1-marble load?

Does a 3-marble load on a 10-coil spring bounce faster or slower than on a 20-coil spring?

With any particular load, do large bounces take a different time from small bounces?

In more detail, a graph may be plotted to show how rate of bouncing varies with the weight on a spring. Marbles (1 to 5) or washers may be used, or more accurate weights. Time, say, 20 bounces of the spring and make a graph of the time for 20 bounces against number of marbles (or washers or the weight in grammes).

How do the graphs for longer and shorter springs differ? Try several to see if there is a relationship.

Note: A bounce is a complete cycle of the spring, up and down, and the time for one bounce is called the *period* which in this case we would measure in seconds.

$$\text{Frequency} = \frac{1}{\text{period}}$$ ie the number of bounces per second.

5. When a spring is bouncing, does the 'trip down' take longer, shorter, or the same time as the 'trip back up'? It will be hard to observe. Use a spring with a long period or match two springs and have one going down while the other is going up.

6. Resonance

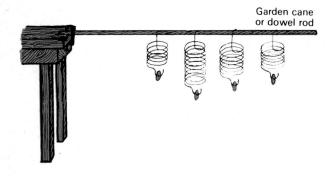

Garden cane
or dowel rod

Can you imagine what the movement of *C* would look like to a fly sitting on *A* ? (Caution: Do not use too large springs for the second and third in the line or the first will be stretched beyond recovery.)

The work on springs will, in some cases, provide a starting point for an interest in waves and wave-motion, and open up a large new area.

First hang a row of springs along the rod. Have some pairs which are equal in number of turns and several single springs which are different. Each should be loaded with one washer. Start each spring vibrating in turn and watch what happens.

Experiment just with two equal springs on the rod.

Does the number of turns matter as long as each spring has the *same* number ?

Does the weight on the spring matter ?

Does it matter where you hang the springs on the rod ?

What happens if you clamp the beam at *both* ends ?

What changes of energy take place when two equal springs are vibrating (with the rod clamped at one end) ?

You may get some interesting things happening if the springs don't quite match.

7. Set up three springs 'in series', with washers between them as shown.

Start *A* moving.

Watch the movement of *C* against a fixed background.

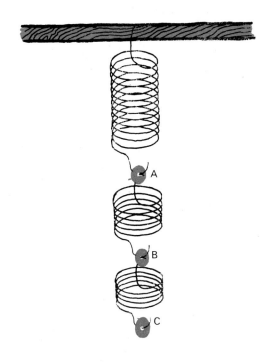

Ball experiments
Another series of investigations which involves both elasticity of materials and energy considerations can be carried out by bouncing balls. This is worked out in the Unit *Science, models and toys,* including a discussion of the variables involved and possible Stage 3 objectives.

Elasticity of other things

Make a list of all the elastic things which give you a
smooth ride in a car. Can you find diagrams of car
suspensions, including Hydrolastic ones?

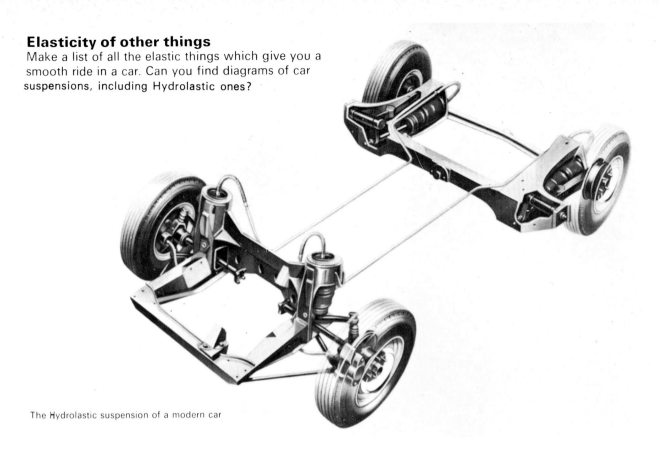

The Hydrolastic suspension of a modern car

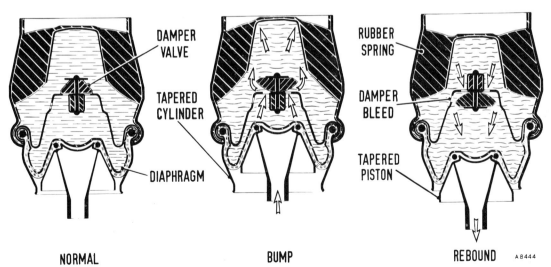

DAMPER
VALVE

TAPERED
CYLINDER

DIAPHRAGM

RUBBER
SPRING

DAMPER
BLEED

TAPERED
PISTON

NORMAL

BUMP

REBOUND

A 8444

Diagram showing the operation of a single Hydrolastic unit

Is air elastic? Is water elastic? The drawing shows how to set up a milk bottle for a party-trick experiment which gives both a surprise and a clue to the answers.

Can you blow air into:

a. The bottle full of water?

b. The bottle half full of water?

How many things do you know which use the elastic property of air? (Pneumatic drills, church organs, hovercraft, tyres, balls, balloons, pop-guns, etc.)

If you think about things which are elastic, does it suggest to you a meaning for the term *'elasticity'*?

Some solid materials are plastic. Quite small forces cause them to flow to take up a new shape and they have so little elasticity that they don't spring back at all but keep the new shape until another force acts on them. Toothpaste and clay are examples. Such materials are often made into the shapes we want by *extruding* them, ie forcing them through a hole. This method is used a great deal in making objects from those plastics materials which are soft when they are warm. They can be forced through holes of different shapes to make lengths of rod or tube which set as they cool. Icing a cake is a kitchen example of extrusion. Can you find examples of things that have been shaped by extrusion?

Apparatus may be designed for extruding Plasticine or clay but the forces required are rather large for class-room experiments. An icing 'pen' used for decorating cakes has been used more successfully. Icing sugar or Dream Topping are pleasant to use in it but the paste made varies in consistency and, of course, sets in time. Vaseline or car grease work well. The various ends provided for the icing pen provide a means of comparing the forces required to push the plastic material through holes of different size and shape and others may be constructed.

Motorway crash barriers
Would lengths of stretched rubber strips make good crash barriers? What are the design factors involved? A good practical investigation would be to design barriers, constructing models and using model cars for testing them. One will need to know about energy (see page 7), strength of materials and elasticity.

What material absorbs a moving car's energy best? Is it possible to use this material for crash barriers? (Putty, clay, Plasticine are hardly practicable.) Is there a best practical compromise? What is the best shape for the material? We have to use a minimum amount of material to keep the cost down, and yet have a barrier strong enough to prevent breakthrough. At the same time we need the maximum absorption of energy so that the car doesn't bounce back too much.

Would it be a good idea to have a sloping barrier? Is there a best angle of slope?

How do all the factors change with different curves of the road?

A deep plastics foam of urea-formaldehyde resin is used to stop aeroplanes which run off the end of runways. Could this be used in the space between motorway lanes? Would a deep layer of gravel work?

Materials under tension
How strong are materials under tension?

Let children devise test apparatus. The most convenient shape in which to have the material is a filament—a wire or a thread.

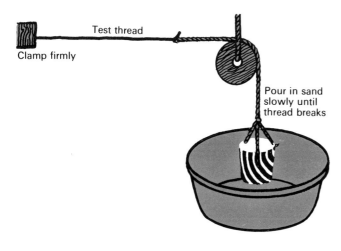

Test thread

Clamp firmly

Pour in sand slowly until thread breaks

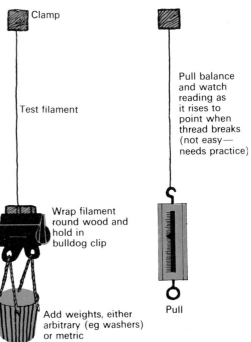

Clamp

Test filament

Wrap filament round wood and hold in bulldog clip

Add weights, either arbitrary (eg washers) or metric

Pull balance and watch reading as it rises to point when thread breaks (not easy—needs practice)

Pull

Some simple ways for testing wires or threads are shown, but it is very important to give children plenty of time to invent their own.

If, particularly with the stronger filaments, there is difficulty in clamping firmly, use the arrangement shown later for testing paper.

Hair

Do people have hair of different strength?

Is there any difference between blond, brunette and red hair; between curly and straight hair; between hair from people of different races; between hair from old people and young people?

Is hair weaker after it has been washed?

Does dyeing or bleaching affect its strength?

Can you identify kinds of hair under the microscope as detectives are supposed to do?

How good a key could you make to the children in your class according to type and strength of hair?

Threads

Compare threads of cotton, linen, silk, wool, Sylko and nylon (from a stocking, a nylon rope or a fishing line). Hemp strands from a rope should also be tried and perhaps very thin fibres stripped from bamboo garden canes. Coconut fibres will sometimes be available. Do the threads have different strengths when they are wet? Why is a rope of hemp or nylon better for towing than steel?

Metals

Try as many wires as can be obtained. TV and radio shops are good sources for wire from old parts and so are car dumps. Different sizes of fuse wire are useful.

In all the tests, as well as comparing strengths, try to notice just *how* the break occurs and the difference in the manner of breaking of different materials.

Paper

Compare all types of paper obtainable with an apparatus such as that shown. Fix the top clamp firmly and hang weights from the bottom clamp.

The weights may be arbitrary ones such as marbles, nails or washers, or standard ones from say 100 g to 1 kg. The most convenient ones are probably slotted weights on a hanger.

What width of paper is a good one to choose for the tests?

Does a tear start usually in the same place?

In practice, test specimens are made as shown in the drawings.

Try these out for testing your paper specimens. What are the advantages?

How does the strength of papers compare with that of metal cooking foil?

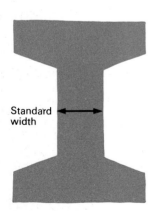

Standard width

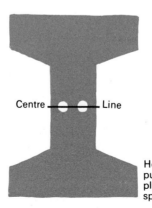

Centre —●● — Line

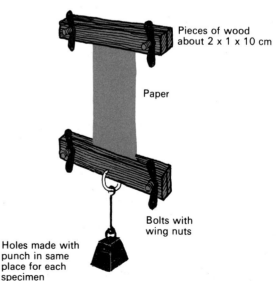

Pieces of wood about 2 x 1 x 10 cm

Paper

Bolts with wing nuts

Holes made with punch in same place for each specimen

Plastics sheet

Cut some strips from a polythene food bag about 2 cm wide. See that the edges are clean-cut. Make marks with a fine felt pen across the strip at $\frac{1}{2}$-cm intervals. Set up the strip for testing in the same way as for paper. Measure the extension for different weights. Draw a graph.

Each time you test, take the weight off again to see how the strip recovers. As the weight on the end increases, does the strip recover equally well? Is the stretch even along the whole length?

Next cut strips from the bag in different directions from the first strip. Do you get the same results with these?

Find different qualities and thicknesses of polythene sheet and test these.

Find other 'stretchy' things (eg Cellophane, old macs, old bathroom curtains) and do the same tests on them.

Tensile strength

It usually seems to take a long time before children think that the cross-section area of the test specimen might matter (most hairs and threads look almost the same anyway). Don't push the matter, but when some children seem ready, introduce two wires of the same metal (eg copper) but of markedly different gauge. You might then need to go back and be more fair about the strength of some people's hair!

Can we decide if a wire 'twice as thick' is twice as strong? By 'twice as thick' do we mean twice the diameter or twice the cross-sectional area?

How can we find the diameter of a wire? Many schools will have micrometers but wire gauge tables may also be used if the gauge of the wire is known.

With several different gauges of wire, plot a graph of the force (weight) needed to break a wire against its diameter. What shape is the graph? Do the two things change in proportion to one another?

Do you get a different shape of graph if you plot the size of force needed to break each wire against the cross-section area of the wire instead of its diameter. Compare the force required for twice the cross-section area, three times the cross-section area and so on. Does any rule begin to appear? Can you use your graph to predict a result?

Standard Wire Gauge table

SWG	Decimal inches	Metric equivalent (mm)
12	0·104	2·642
13	0·092	2·337
14	0·080	2·032
15	0·072	1·829
16	0·064	1·626
17	0·056	1·422
18	0·048	1·219
19	0·040	1·016
20	0·036	0·914
21	0·032	0·813
22	0·028	0·711
23	0·024	0·610
24	0·022	0·559
25	0·020	0·508
26	0·018	0·457
27	0·0164	0·416
28	0·0149	0·376
29	0·0136	0·345
30	0·0124	0·315
31	0·0116	0·294
32	0·0108	0·274
33	0·0100	0·254
34	0·0092	0·233
35	0·0084	0·213
36	0·0076	0·193

Reinforcing

Concrete is strong enough in compression but fairly weak in tension so concrete beams are often cast with steel rods in them where they are needed to withstand tensile stresses.

Cast some small concrete beams (about $30 \times 2 \times 2$ cm), some from plain concrete mix and others with reinforcing wires. Clamp one end and load the other to compare their breaking strengths.

In buildings, the reinforcement is positioned where there is to be *tension* in the beam. Where there is compression it is not needed. A beam for a balcony is reinforced in a different place from a beam for a floor.

Casting prestressed concrete beams for Newbury road-over-rail bridge, Berkshire *(below)*. A prestressed concrete T-beam during the construction of Crowbridge viaduct, Glamorgan *(opposite)*.

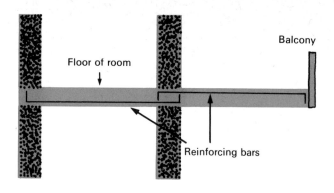

Less steel is needed if the wires are prestressed. To do this ducts are left in the concrete and steel wires are fed through. These are stressed by pulling the ends while the holes are filled up with cement under pressure When the cement has set the stress is taken off the wires which now pull the concrete together, compressing it. A load on the beam is balanced first by this compression before it even begins to cause a tension and so the beam can take more load than with ordinary reinforcing which is not stressed. The Medway road bridge in Kent is a fine example of the use of prestressed concrete. It has the largest concrete cantilever ever made.

Some more tests for materials (particularly suitable for plastics)*

Softening point

Some plastics soften when they are warmed. Do all thermoplastics soften at the same temperature? Softening point tests may be done as shown:

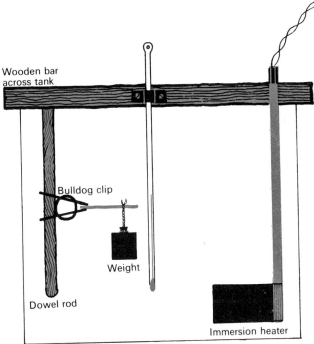

Wooden bar across tank

Bulldog clip

Weight

Dowel rod

Immersion heater

Clamp test specimen between two pieces of wood or metal in a strong bulldog clip or other clamp

The immersion heater is not a necessity, and the kind of tank is not very important, a saucepan of water heated gently on a gas ring would do. A standard size specimen should be decided on, say 5 cm × 5 mm × 1 mm and the weight used might be about 20 g.

There is another Unit called Children and plastics
Stages 1 & 2 and Background.

Creep

Measure amount of bending for different specimens (again choose a standard size). Leave the apparatus set up and record bend over several days to measure any 'creep'. Then take the weight off and record how the strip recovers. Does it go back completely? Does it return any further if you leave it for a day or two?

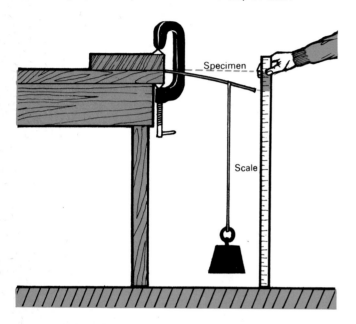

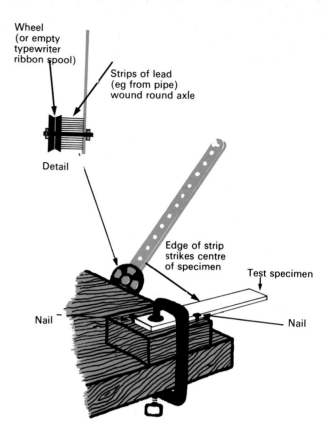

Wheel (or empty typewriter ribbon spool)

Strips of lead (eg from pipe) wound round axle

Detail

Edge of strip strikes centre of specimen

Test specimen

Nail

Nail

Impact test

In the earlier stages children will have devised impact tests for materials. Usually they will have dropped weights of various sizes from the same height on to the material to be tested. Perhaps there will be a need at this stage for more sophistication. Should the specimen be of standard size? Does it matter how it is supported while it is being struck? An apparatus of the kind shown on the drawing could be used.

The angle from which the pendulum is released is slowly increased until the impact breaks the specimen. The impact-resisting strengths of different plastics may be compared by comparing this angle for each of them.

It is important to have a rigid arm for the pendulum and that the weights on the pendulum and the sample being tested are fixed firmly.

Children might well devise a similar impact tester from a weighted trolley running down a slope in place of the pendulum.

Hardness

A good way of comparing the hardness of materials is to clamp a ball-bearing between two pieces of each material in a vice, first adjusting the vice so that the ball just does not fall through and then giving a standard number of turns to the screw. The depths (or diameters) of the dents produced are compared.

As well as comparing plastics with wood and metals, materials like papier mache and fibre-glass may be tried. An even easier way is to use an automatic punch (see Appendix). This is 'fired' on test materials and the sizes of the holes punched are compared.

The surfaces of liquids

If you try to pull apart the surface of a liquid (for example, if you try to make an object go through from the air to the liquid or pull it out of the liquid into the air) there is a pull back along the surface of the liquid, ie there is a tension. It is called surface tension. The liquid acts for all the world as if it had a skin on the top. This is a common enough experience and has many everyday manifestations and applications.

Animals

One of the best starting experiences is to watch animals on the surface of ponds, ditches and puddles. Water skaters (*Gerris*) and whirligig beetles (*Gyrinus*) are common.

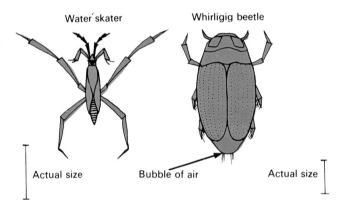

Water skater   Whirligig beetle

Actual size   Bubble of air   Actual size

How exactly do they move?

What are they doing?

Why do they come out more on sunny days?

Look for the dips in the surface under the feet of the water skaters and find how the surface goes to hold up the whirligig beetle.

What is the silvery ball at the rear end of the beetle?

How do these animals react to shadows passing over them?

Other insects moving on the water surface might be the water cricket (*Velia*) or the water measurer (*Hydrometrica*). The bank spiders which are not water animals at all will often also run out along the surface after their prey.

If these animals are kept in an aquarium a fine-mesh nylon cover must be kept over it and water plants and stones should come up out of the water to provide a refuge and a simulated bank.

Look for mosquito and gnat larvae and pupae. They are common in summer on any stagnant water. How do they use the surface skin? How do they breathe?

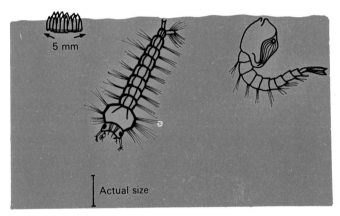

1.   Yellow eggs   2. Larva   3. Pupa

5 mm

Actual size

If a gnat egg-raft is collected it may be kept in a jam jar of water and the whole sequence of development watched very conveniently.

How are mosquito pests attacked in tropical countries?

In a school aquarium it is a common sight to see the water snails crawling from one side to another clinging to the underside of the surface 'skin' of the water. How do water snails breathe? Do they have to come to the surface?

69

Leaves

Look at lupin leaves after rain. How big is the biggest drop which collects in the centre? (How are you going to measure it?) Why doesn't the water run away between the leaflets?

What shape and size of water drops can you make on other kinds of leaf?

How could you do an experiment to find out whether water soaks into leaves?

Some simple effects of surface tension

Everyone knows about floating a needle on water. You can't do it if the needle is clean but if you stroke one with your fingers there is usually enough grease to stop

the water wetting the steel and so it can be floated with care. A razor blade is much easier.

Try a paper-clip and some steel wool.

Look closely at the surface near the floating object and make an enlarged sketch of how the surface goes.

Sieves made from metal gauze or perforated zinc may be floated and other things to try would be: iron filings, dry tea leaves, dried peas and strips of aluminium foil.

Use a medicine dropper (pipette) to add drops of liquid detergent or soap solution to find the smallest number of drops required to sink each of the floating objects.

There are many other small experiments to demonstrate surface tension effects, for example:

a. The can has two small holes drilled 5 mm apart in its base.

Streams of water

Fill with water and hold over a sink.

With the fingers, twist the jets together.

Why do they stay like this?

b. Weight the wire frame so that it floats with the ring about 1 cm above the surface of water.

Push it under and let it rise gently.

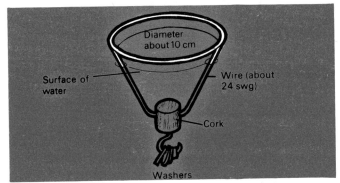

Why doesn't it come up again? Look at the surface of the water near the ring.

Tilt the ring. What happens now?

c. 'Fill' a jar with water and then very carefully add more and more. How far can you go? What holds the extra water up?

Another way is to fill the jar and then see how many coins you can gently slip in without spilling any water.

d. Look at the bristles of a paint brush first under water and then when you pull it out. What causes the difference?

e. Pour water along a rod.

What holds it on? Is there any difference between rods of different material? Glass, metal, plastics and wood may be tried.

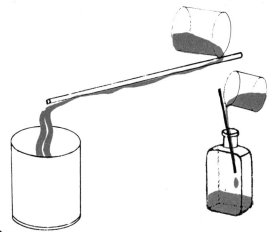

Drops
What shape are the drops coming from a slowly dripping tap? What holds them together? Put some single drops of water on a post-card. Look closely and draw their shape. What is the biggest drop you can make without it bursting? Are the large drops the same shape as the small ones?

Try making water drops on many different surfaces, for example, glass, wood, metals, many kinds of card and paper, different kinds of cloth, greasy or waxy surfaces.

What about liquids other than water (eg methylated spirit, cooking oil, paraffin, turpentine)? Why do you get different results? Three other Units give help with further ideas: *Change Stages 1 & 2, Holes, gaps and cavities,* and *Early experiences.* Although *Early experiences* is for infant work the ideas can be developed to quite a sophisticated level.

Different liquids
Is there a different tension in the surface of different liquids?

a. Give the surface of some water a light dusting of talcum powder. Drop on to the water one spot of meths, detergent solution or soap solution. Have these liquids a higher or lower surface tension than water?

b. Just cover the bottom of a dish with water. Drop a spot or two of meths or liquid detergent in the middle.

What makes the 'island' form? Why does the water creep back again after a time?

c. Make camphor boats. The shape may be cut from old photograph negatives (this will not stick to the sides of a dish). Make the boat 2 or 3 cm long.

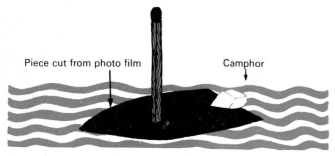

Piece cut from photo film   Camphor

Fix a piece of camphor in the notch at the back and put the boat on very clean water in a very clean bowl.

What makes the boat go? (Camphor is soluble in water.)

Is the surface tension of camphor solution bigger or less than that of water? Will the boat go with a little detergent powder put at the back instead of camphor?

If the boat stops, change the water and give the bowl an extra clean.

d. Make a loop of thread and float it on water.

Drop a spot of detergent or soap solution in the centre of the loop. How do you explain what happens?

What happens if you put the spot of detergent *outside* the loop?

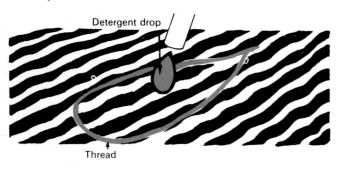

Detergent drop

Thread

e. Try a 'delayed action tug-of-war'. Put 2 or 3 ml of cooking oil on to water in a dish and then one drop of soap or detergent solution in the centre on top.

Try the effect of other liquids dropped on one another in a similar way.

The effect of temperature
Dust the surface of some water with talcum powder. Touch it with a hot rod. Why does it clear? What happens when you remove the rod? Why does it happen? If you start with *hot* water does it make any difference?

Measuring surface tension
A simple home-made balance is needed. As with the force-measurers and timers in the first part of this Unit, there is good sense in letting children have plenty of time to design, construct and test their own.

A simple light wooden beam with a needle for a pivot works quite well. A second way to support the beam is also shown in the drawing. The degree to which the panel pins are driven in affects the sensitivity of the balance so one has some control over this.

Notice the counterweight (conveniently made of an inverted U-shape of thick copper wire). This is moved to a position which makes the beam level before each experiment starts.

a. Cut a piece of paper as shown and suspend from one arm of the balance.

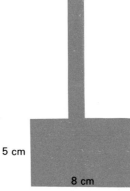

5 cm

8 cm

First bring the dry 8 cm edge in contact with the water in a dish and watch what happens.

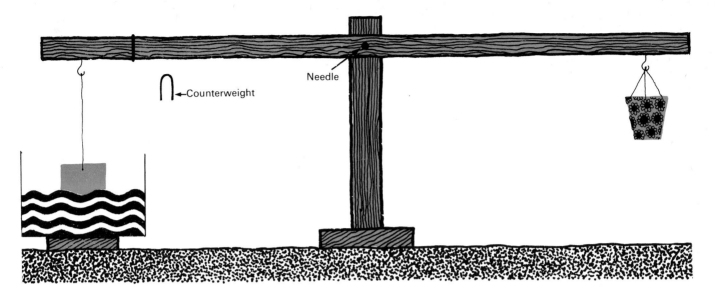

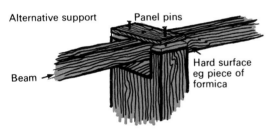

Alternative support   Panel pins

Beam   Hard surface eg piece of formica

Then wet the whole paper rectangle, arrange the dish of water so that the lower edge of paper is just in contact with the water surface and find the pull needed to get it out.

Washers make good weights.

b. Cut a square plate shape from some stiff plastics material.

About 5 cm

Make a hole in the centre and a paper-clip hook to go through it.

With the simple balance find how many washers are needed to pull the plate out of a water surface. (Start with the balance arm level.)

Does it matter how much water you have in the dish? Does the shape or size of the dish of water matter? What happens if the plate isn't clean? Can you try other liquids (soapy water, methylated spirits, cooking oil, etc)?

Does the shape of the plate matter? Does the area of the plate matter? Does the circumference matter?

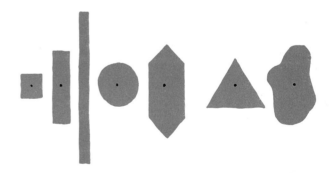

With plates such as those shown in the drawing, graph:

Number of washers/area of plate

Number of washers/circumference of plate

Do either of the graphs show any relationship?

How do wire rings compare with plates?

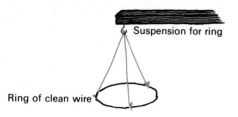

Suspension for ring

Ring of clean wire

c. Can you use the apparatus to measure how surface tension changes with temperature? Make a graph.

d. Use it too to find the effect of different strengths of detergent solutions on the surface tension of water. Liquid detergents are the easiest to use but solutions of washing powders could be tried too. A *very* little detergent makes a lot of difference so it is best to start with very weak solutions and gradually increase the strength. (A plate which has been contaminated with detergent needs a *very* thorough washing in plain water for a long time before it can give sensible readings again, so it is very difficult to start with strong solutions and work downwards.) Make a graph to show how surface tension changes with amount of detergent used and use it to find the most economical strength of detergent solution to use for washing up.

Do all detergents sold give the same result?

Is there a best buy?

Is it true that most people use far too much detergent for washing up?

Do the washing machine instructions tell us to use more detergent than necessary and so aggravate the pollution problem?

No doubt this will set off an investigation into washing powder advertising. Is there really one which washes whiter than the others? The investigation is well worth doing as an exercise in thinking out and controlling variables. Equally dirty pieces of the same cloth, the same kind of dirt or stain, equal quantities of detergent, equal temperatures, equal times of washing, equal rinsing and the same *method* of washing are all necessary.

How do you judge in the end? Do you take people's opinion? If so, how many people have to agree on the order of whiteness of the test pieces before you think an answer is valid? Could a camera exposure-meter help?

If you do get a result, is the order of preference for the different products different when they are tested for different stains? Are 'biological' powders the best for some kinds of stain and dirt?

Enzymes, which the biological powders contain, are very sensitive to temperature. Can you find out how well an enzyme powder works for different temperatures of the washing water with, say, bloodstains or fruit juice or beetroot stains? Is there a clear-cut best temperature?

If children know about acidity (they may have used a soil tester for example) they might continue tests for enzyme powders using washing water made up to different pH values as tested by indicator paper (see Appendix). Enzymes are sensitive to the acidity of their surroundings. At which pH do the enzyme powders work best?

Capillarity

Cut a strip of blotting paper or paper towel about 3 cm wide. Hang it vertically with the lower end dipping in water. How *fast* does the water rise? Does it slow up as it gets higher? How high will it finally rise?

Why does the water do this? Look at the blotting paper, especially a torn edge, with a lens.

Set up the experiments shown in the drawings.

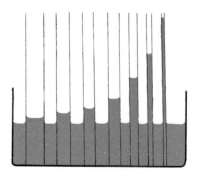

Tubes of different diameters, including some very fine ones are placed vertically in water. (Give them a good wetting first.)

Glass tubes, plastic tubes from ball-point pens, straws, etc, may be used.

How high does the water rise up the tube?

How does the height seem to depend on the diameter of the tube?

Does the material of which the tube is made make any difference?

Wet two glass plates (cover glasses for photo slides) and stand them up in water as shown.

Make a sketch of what you see between the plates.

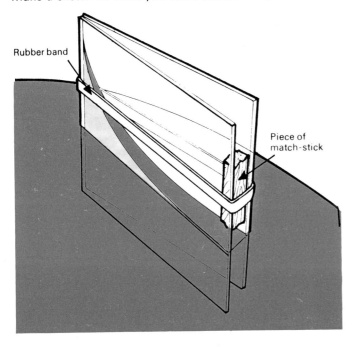

Rubber band

Piece of match-stick

If a liquid wets a tube, the surface tension pull lifts up a column of liquid.

The narrower the tube, the higher the column of liquid.

The angle of contact of the liquid with the tube depends on what the tube is made of, what the liquid is and whether the tube is clean.

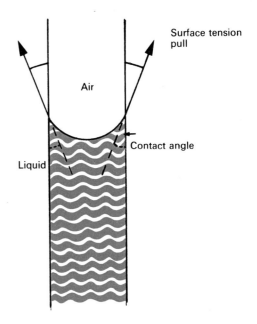

Surface tension pull

Air

Contact angle

Liquid

Previous experiments could be tried with liquids other than water (different tube materials have already been suggested). A greasy tube may be compared with a clean one of equal diameter in the same liquid and so on.

Towels and blotting paper are made of fibres which act like narrow tubes. Find out how water rises up strips of many *kinds* of paper and also try strips of different *widths*. (Evaporation from the edges may make a difference.)

Next try different kinds of cloth: for example, towelling and other cotton cloth, woollen cloth, silk, nylon, linen. Which is the best for drying yourself on and which the worst? Use a lens or microscope to try to find out why.

Will different liquids rise up a strip of blotting paper at the same rate? Paraffin, cooking oil, methylated spirit, different strengths of washing up liquid, vinegar and so on may be tried.

Simple chromatography experiments may be set up:

Quink black ink is a good thing to start with, but the whole work should be an investigation on the part of the children.

Try different inks, coffee, strong tea, laundry blue, water soluble dyes, the juice from red cabbage, Boots' 'edible green' and other food colourants.

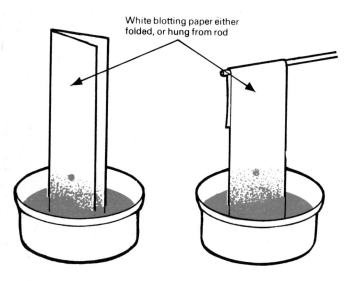

White blotting paper either folded, or hung from rod

A group of well-advanced children in a school with some laboratory facilities could take this investigation a good deal further. *They might use alcohol (industrial spirit) or acetone (or a mixture of both) as solvents in addition to water. Then they could investigate the inks used in ballpoint pens and the colours in plant petals and leaves. (A good source of chlorophyll is the spinach sold in tins for feeding young children.)

An interest in dyes may follow and there is some help on this topic in the Unit *Coloured things*.

*See article 'Chromatography for Junior Schools' in School Science Review, no. 179 (December 1970).

Soils

Try the capillarity effect in different soils. Get samples of clay soil, loamy soil and sandy soil. Dry and powder them, picking out any stones. Pack each sample to a depth of about 50 cm in a transparent plastic tube about 10–15 mm diameter. (These are now quite easily obtained from garages and 'Do-it-Yourself' shops.)

A piece of muslin tied round the base of the tube holds the soil in, and this end is dipped into water with the tube held vertically. The rise in water can be watched and timed. If the three kinds of soil are set up together to 'race', it will be found to be a hare and tortoise affair, the clay starting very slowly but 'winning' by rising to the greatest height in the end. Soils from different localities should be compared in this way.

How important is this water raising capacity of soil for plant growth? Different kinds of dry soil are placed in deep pots which stand in water. If seeds are planted near the surface, or equally strong plants of the same species planted in the pots, one can get some idea of the effect of capillarity but it is difficult to be 'fair' with plant material and not only would the same test have to be done many times, preferably with different groups of people, but also with different plant species and different samples of sand, loam and clay because the chemical content of the soil may have more effect than its water-raising capability. It is all good practical science training!

One reason why loam is ideal for plant growth is that it is not far behind clay in its capilliary capabilities and in addition drains well and does not become water-logged as clay does. Roots respire as well as the rest of a plant and this cannot take place if all the spaces between soil particles are filled with water.

Structures and patterns

In order to have space to develop ideas about forces, little development has been made in this Stage 3 part of the Unit on the subject of structures and patterns. Teachers could very well develop their own 'units' on some of the following lines:

Strength related to structure in stems and roots.

The structure of flowers and seeds.

Crystals.

Bubbles and foam.

Geological structure: rocks and soils.

Waves and wave patterns.

Patterns of life.

Animal behaviour patterns.

What about objectives?

Objectives have been inherent in all work described and this seems a good point at which to discuss them. An explanation of objectives and a detailed list is included at the end of the Unit.

They seem to group themselves into three types:

1. First there are many objectives which can only be expressed by the teacher intimately concerned with the actual conditions. They are specific to the teaching situation and the needs of particular children.

2. Secondly there are those, mainly included in the column *attitudes, interests and aesthetic awareness* in the statment of Objectives at the end of the book, which would be appropriate to all the activities described in this Unit. Has any progress towards these been achieved?

3. A third group consists of those objectives more related to the subject matter. It might help to state these in more detail and they are listed below.

It would be inappropriate for a teacher to feel that all the work in the Unit and all the objectives in this list had to be 'covered' like the syllabus for an examination. Some objectives will be attained by some of the children.

Different objectives will almost certainly have to be revised by the teacher after the work has started. For example it may be found that, when looking at falling objects, the effect of air resistance is the most interesting factor for one or more groups of children, leading them to some detailed study of flight or fluid flow. In this case many objectives, particularly those concerned with acquiring knowledge will be different ones from any listed here. All we would hope is that a teacher will from time to time consider what the objectives are, taking those of ours as samples, and reckon up how far they have been attained.

Examples of objectives appropriate to this Unit

Observing, exploring and ordering observations
Awareness of common effects of frictional forces.

Awareness of ways in which objects fall to the ground.

Awareness of the typical shape of the path of a projectile.

Awareness of some common physical properties of fluids (both gases and liquids), eg viscosity.

Awareness of some common repetitive motions.

Developing basic concepts and logical thinking
Familiarity with distance/time relationships: velocity acceleration.

Ability to separate, exclude or combine variables in approaching problems.

Posing questions and devising investigations to answer them
Ability to attempt to define a problem and identify essential steps in the scientific approach to it.

Ability to design experiments with effective controls for testing hypotheses.

Ability to visualise 'perfect conditions' in order to derive a useful simplification of actual observations (eg movement with NO friction).

Use of models for investigating causal relations.

Acquiring knowledge and learning skills
Knowledge of some common forms of energy.

Knowledge that energy can be stored in a variety of ways.

Awareness that one way to measure a force is by its effect in deforming materials.

Some familiarity with the idea of work being derived from energy-changes and how work can be measured: that power is the rate of doing work.

Awareness that if a force moves a mass it causes it to accelerate.

Appreciation of the idea of momentum.

Knowledge of the lives and some of the work of Newton and Galileo.

Ability to devise, make and use simple apparatus.

Experimental ability to control variables.

Ability to collect and record quantitative results.

Awareness of the effects of tension and compression forces on materials.

Awareness of the presence of a tension in the surface of liquids and of some of its effects.

Here it should be stressed again that we want the awareness, knowledge and skill to come from much practical experience over a considerable time, experience normally of practical conditions which will not be perfect and so where a perfect simplified mathematical relationship may not be true. The idea that a simplification, a look at what might happen under hypothetically perfect conditions is a useful scientific 'thinking tool', is one we would like our Stage 3 children to come across by this means.

Communicating
Selection of appropriate graphical form to suit information.

Ability to deduce information from graphs and tabulated results.

Awareness of the need to develop international standard units of measurement.

Interpreting findings critically
Ability to interpret results, ie to draw conclusions from unbiased observations.

Willingness to accept factual evidence despite perceptual contradictions.

Some awareness of the need to estimate degree of accuracy of measurements and that rough measurements may be useful as long as the degree of accuracy is always kept in mind.

Appreciating patterns and relationships
Appreciation of social implications of man's changing use of power.

Recognition that energy has many forms and can be changed from one to another.

Awareness of conservation in energy transformations.

Awareness of the universal nature of gravity.

Appreciation of pattern of movement in the solar system.

Appreciation of repetitive patterns in some simple harmonic motions.

Appendix

Apparatus and equipment notes

Almost all materials can be obtained from ordinary school supplies or collected from scrap but the following information about some items may be helpful.

Automatic punches (for hardness testing)
Made by 'Eclipse' and may be bought at tool shops.

Balance, 5 kg with hook
Nuffield O-level Item 85 is a good one.

Camphor squares
From chemists.

Earphones
Must be *low* resistance. From radio shops, advertisers in *Wireless World* or Griffin & George Item 83–660 (much more expensive).

Elastic cords
Shirring elastic for small trolleys. Nuffield Item 106/2 Square-section, eg 4 mm or 6 mm from model shops.

Electric motors
Orbit motors (distributors are Ripmax). From model shops. There is a series of five with different powers.

Immersion heater (6-V and 12-V models)
Often advertised in *Wireless World* and *Practical Electronics* or Nuffield Item 75 from laboratory suppliers.

Indicator papers (for testing acidity)
Available as soil testers from Boots or use Universal Indicator Books (Philip Harris C1766).

Magnets
Ring magnets (ceramic), E. J. Arnold KN649. Short cylindrical (and others) Eclipse magnets from tool shops and ironmongers.

Metronome
A good reasonably priced one is the Taktell, E. J. Arnold KB 055001.

Plastics tubing (transparent)
The wider sizes are sold by garages; finer tubes from model shops.

Polystyrene beads
Philip Harris P7957. Styrocell beads (larger), P7957/05

Propellors
Two- and three- bladed, plastic. From model aeroplane shops.

Radiometer
Toy departments, stores such as Habitat or E. J. Arnold SM440

Slinky springs
From toyshops or E. J. Arnold KN851.

Springs (wide steel)
Item 2 from Nuffield O-level 'elastic materials kit' are useful for force-measurers or buffers.

Syringe (plastic, 5 ml)
Nuffield Item 6D.

Wire
Constantan (often called eureka) Philip Harris P6884

about 24-gauge would be suitable.

Iron wire
Sold by BDH on 1-oz reels (about 35 SWG) so a branch of Boots could obtain it. For thick iron wire use florist's wire from ironmongers.

Piano wire
Obtainable from model shops, 14- and 16-gauge are most useful.

Wheels
Keil Kraft 38-mm (1½-in) diameter.

Bibliography

Nuffield Secondary Science Project, Theme 6, *Movement.*

Nuffield Combined Sciences, *Teachers' Guide I,* Section 2.

Tricker, R. H. R. and B. J. K., *The Science of Movement,* Mills & Boon.

Gray, James, *How Animals Move,* CUP or Penguin.

Sterland, E. G., *Energy into Power,* Aldus Books.

Unilever Education Booklet, *Surface Activity.*

The Jackdaw on *Isaac Newton.*

Boys, C. V., *Soap Bubbles,* Heinemann, 1960.

To make the coils for apparatus on page 11

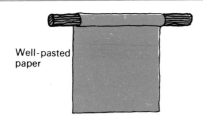

Well-pasted paper

Cut a strip of duplicating paper about 5 cm by 20 cm.

Paste it thoroughly with wallpaper paste. Wrap it round a dowel rod (or pencil, etc) which is a little larger in diameter than the magnet to be used.

Slide the resulting cylinder off while still wet and allow to dry. It will be quite hard.

Cut card discs to make a tight push-on fit. Paste a very narrow strip of paper about 5 cm long and wind it round as shown to prevent the disc from being pushed outwards as the wire is wound on.

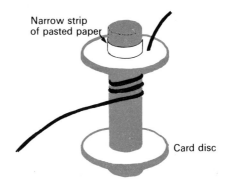

Narrow strip of pasted paper

Card disc

The ends of the central tube may be made neat by trimming with a small Eclipse hack-saw.

Start winding by pushing a length of wire through a pin-hole near the core. Finish off the coil by pushing the other end of the wire through a pin-hole near the outer edge of a disc.

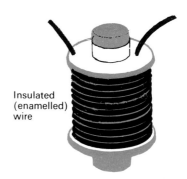

Insulated (enamelled) wire

Balsa wood trolley (approx half size)

Materials
Orbit electric motors. Use range: 305, 405, 505. (Although the suggested range of voltages for these varies it has been found quite safe to work all of them on 4·5 V for short periods.)

Battery, 4·5-V (Ever Ready 1289).

Three Keil Kraft wheels, 3·8-cm (1½-in) diameter (approx.).

No. 14 piano wire.

Balsa-wood sheet 6 or 7 mm (¼ in) thick.

Balsa cement.

Model aeroplane propellers (two or three blades) to fit motors.

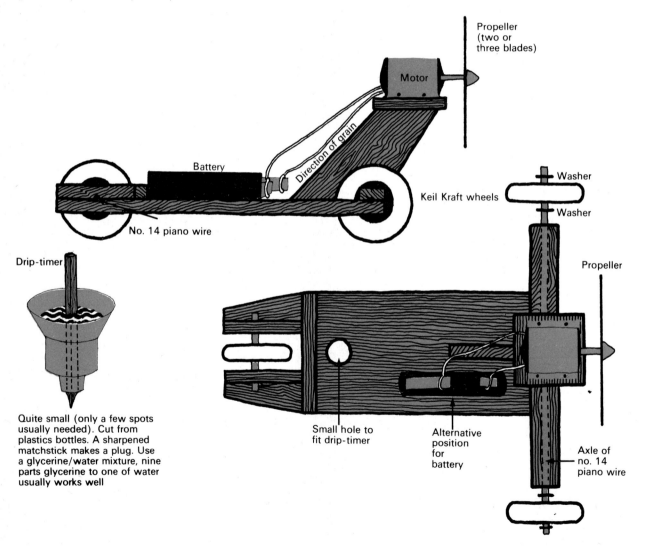

Propeller (two or three blades)

Motor

Direction of grain

Battery

No. 14 piano wire

Keil Kraft wheels

Washer

Washer

Propeller

Drip-timer

Quite small (only a few spots usually needed). Cut from plastics bottles. A sharpened matchstick makes a plug. Use a glycerine/water mixture, nine parts glycerine to one of water usually works well

Small hole to fit drip-timer

Alternative position for battery

Axle of no. 14 piano wire

Objectives for children learning science

Guide lines to keep in mind

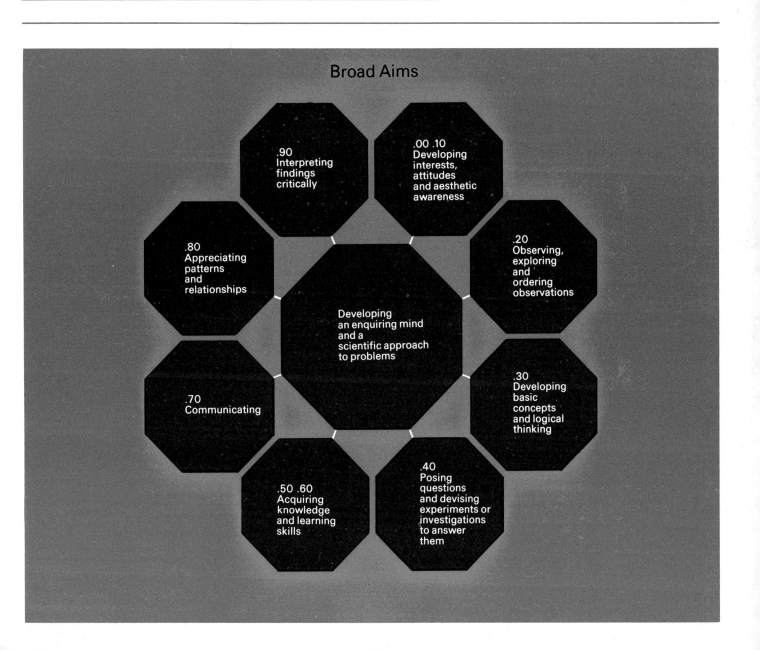

Broad Aims

.90
Interpreting
findings
critically

.00 .10
Developing
interests,
attitudes
and aesthetic
awareness

.80
Appreciating
patterns
and
relationships

.20
Observing,
exploring
and
ordering
observations

Developing
an enquiring mind
and a
scientific approach
to problems

.70
Communicating

.30
Developing
basic
concepts
and logical
thinking

.50 .60
Acquiring
knowledge
and learning
skills

.40
Posing
questions
and devising
experiments or
investigations
to answer
them

What we mean by Stage 1, Stage 2 and Stage 3

Attitudes, interests and aesthetic awareness

.00/.10

Stage 1
Transition from intuition to concrete operations. Infants generally.

The characteristics of thought among infant children differ in important respects from those of children over the age of about seven years. Infant thought has been described as 'intuitive' by Piaget; it is closely associated with physical action and is dominated by immediate observation. Generally, the infant is not able to think about or imagine the consequences of an action unless he has actually carried it out, nor is he yet likely to draw logical conclusions from his experiences. At this early stage the objectives are those concerned with active exploration of the immediate environment and the development of ability to discuss and communicate effectively: they relate to the kind of activities that are appropriate to these very young children, and which form an introduction to ways of exploring and of ordering observations.

1.01 Willingness to ask questions
1.02 Willingness to handle both living and non-living material.
1.03 Sensitivity to the need for giving proper care to living things.
1.04 Enjoyment in using all the senses for exploring and discriminating.
1.05 Willingness to collect material for observation or investigation.

Concrete operations. Early stage.

In this Stage, children are developing the ability to manipulate things mentally. At first this ability is limited to objects and materials that can be manipulated concretely, and even then only in a restricted way. The objectives here are concerned with developing these mental operations through exploration of concrete objects and materials—that is to say, objects and materials which, as physical things, have meaning for the child. Since older children, and even adults prefer an introduction to new ideas and problems through concrete example and physical exploration, these objectives are suitable for all children, whatever their age, who are being introduced to certain science activities for the first time.

1.06 Desire to find out things for oneself.
1.07 Willing participation in group work.
1.08 Willing compliance with safety regulations in handling tools and equipment.
1.09 Appreciation of the need to learn the meaning of new words and to use them correctly.

Stage 2
Concrete operations. Later stage.

In this Stage, a continuation of what Piaget calls the stage of concrete operations, the mental manipulations are becoming more varied and powerful. The developing ability to handle variables—for example, in dealing with multiple classification—means that problems can be solved in more ordered and quantitative ways than was previously possible. The objectives begin to be more specific to the exploration of the scientific aspects of the environment rather than to general experience, as previously. These objectives are developments of those of Stage 1 and depend on them for a foundation. They are those thought of as being appropriate for all children who have progressed from Stage 1 and not merely for nine- to eleven-year-olds.

2.01 Willingness to co-operate with others in science activities.
2.02 Willingness to observe objectively.
2.03 Appreciation of the reasons for safety regulations.
2.04 Enjoyment in examining ambiguity in the use of words.
2.05 Interest in choosing suitable means of expressing results and observations.
2.06 Willingness to assume responsibility for the proper care of living things.
2.07 Willingness to examine critically the results of their own and others' work.
2.08 Preference for putting ideas to test before accepting or rejecting them.
2.09 Appreciation that approximate methods of comparison may be more appropriate than careful measurements.

Stage 3
Transition to stage of abstract thinking.

This is the Stage in which, for some children, the ability to think about abstractions is developing. When this development is complete their thought is capable of dealing with the possible and hypothetical, and is not tied to the concrete and to the here and now. It may take place between eleven and thirteen for some able children, for some children it may happen later, and for others it may never occur. The objectives of this stage are ones which involve development of ability to use hypothetical reasoning and to separate and combine variables in a systematic way. They are appropriate to those who have achieved most of the Stage 2 objectives and who now show signs of ability to manipulate mentally ideas and propositions.

3.01 Acceptance of responsibility for their own and others' safety in experiments.
3.02 Preference for using words correctly.
3.03 Commitment to the idea of physical cause and effect.
3.04 Recognition of the need to standardise measurements.
3.05 Willingness to examine evidence critically.
3.06 Willingness to consider beforehand the usefulness of the results from a possible experiment.
3.07 Preference for choosing the most appropriate means of expressing results or observations.
3.08 Recognition of the need to acquire new skills.
3.09 Willingness to consider the role of science in everyday life.

Attitudes, interests and aesthetic awareness

.00/.10

1.11 Awareness that there are various ways of testing out ideas and making observations.
1.12 Interest in comparing and classifying living or non-living things.
1.13 Enjoyment in comparing measurements with estimates.
1.14 Awareness that there are various ways of expressing results and observations.
1.15 Willingness to wait and to keep records in order to observe change in things.
1.16 Enjoyment in exploring the variety of living things in the environment.
1.17 Interest in discussing and comparing the aesthetic qualities of materials.

2.11 Enjoyment in developing methods for solving problems or testing ideas.
2.12 Appreciation of the part that aesthetic qualities of materials play in determining their use.
2.13 Interest in the way discoveries were made in the past.

3.11 Appreciation of the main principles in the care of living things.
3.12 Willingness to extend methods used in science activities to other fields of experience.

Observing, exploring and ordering observations

.20

1.21 Appreciation of the variety of living things and materials in the environment.
1.22 Awareness of changes which take place as time passes.
1.23 Recognition of common shapes—square, circle, triangle.
1.24 Recognition of regularity in patterns.
1.25 Ability to group things consistently according to chosen or given criteria.

1.26 Awareness of the structure and form of living things.
1.27 Awareness of change of living things and non-living materials.
1.28 Recognition of the action of force
1.29 Ability to group living and non-living things by observable attributes.
1.29a Ability to distinguish regularity in events and motion.

2.21 Awareness of internal structure in living and non-living things.
2.22 Ability to construct and use keys for identification.
2.23 Recognition of similar and congruent shapes.
2.24 Awareness of symmetry in shapes and structures.
2.25 Ability to classify living things and non-living materials in different ways.
2.26 Ability to visualise objects from different angles and the shape of cross-sections.

3.21 Appreciation that classification criteria are arbitrary.
3.22 Ability to distinguish observations which are relevant to the solution of a problem from those which are not.
3.23 Ability to estimate the order of magnitude of physical quantities.

	Developing basic concepts and logical thinking .30	**Posing questions and devising experiments or investigations to answer them** .40
Stage 1 Transition from intuition to concrete operations. Infants generally.	*1.31* Awareness of the meaning of words which describe various types of quantity. *1.32* Appreciation that things which are different may have features in common.	*1.41* Ability to find answers to simple problems by investigation. *1.42* Ability to make comparisons in terms of one property or variable.
Concrete operations. Early stage.	*1.33* Ability to predict the effect of certain changes through observation of similar changes. *1.34* Formation of the notions of the horizontal and the vertical. *1.35* Development of concepts of conservation of length and substance. *1.36* Awareness of the meaning of speed and of its relation to distance covered.	*1.43* Appreciation of the need for measurement. *1.44* Awareness that more than one variable may be involved in a particular change.
Stage 2 Concrete operations. Later stage.	*2.31* Appreciation of measurement as division into regular parts and repeated comparison with a unit. *2.32* Appreciation that comparisons can be made indirectly by use of an intermediary. *2.33* Development of concepts of conservation of weight, area and volume. *2.34* Appreciation of weight as a downward force. *2.35* Understanding of the speed, time, distance relation.	*2.41* Ability to frame questions likely to be answered through investigations. *2.42* Ability to investigate variables and to discover effective ones. *2.43* Appreciation of the need to control variables and use controls in investigations. *2.44* Ability to choose and use either arbitrary or standard units of measurement as appropriate. *2.45* Ability to select a suitable degree of approximation and work to it. *2.46* Ability to use representational models for investigating problems or relationships.
Stage 3 Transition to stage of abstract thinking.	*3.31* Familiarity with relationships involving velocity, distance, time, acceleration. *3.32* Ability to separate, exclude or combine variables in approaching problems. *3.33* Ability to formulate hypotheses not dependent upon direct observation. *3.34* Ability to extend reasoning beyond the actual to the possible. *3.35* Ability to distinguish a logically sound proof from others less sound.	*3.41* Attempting to identify the essential steps in approaching a problem scientifically. *3.42* Ability to design experiments with effective controls for testing hypotheses. *3.43* Ability to visualise a hypothetical situation as a useful simplification of actual observations. *3.44* Ability to construct scale models for investigation and to appreciate implications of changing the scale.

1.51 Ability to discriminate between different materials.
1.52 Awareness of the characteristics of living things.
1.53 Awareness of properties which materials can have.
1.54 Ability to use displayed reference material for identifying living and non-living things.

1.55 Familiarity with sources of sound.
1.56 Awareness of sources of heat, light and electricity.
1.57 Knowledge that change can be produced in common substances.
1.58 Appreciation that ability to move or cause movement requires energy.
1.59 Knowledge of differences in properties between and within common groups of materials.

1.61 Appreciation of man's use of other living things and their products.
1.62 Awareness that man's way of life has changed through the ages.
1.63 Skill in manipulating tools and materials.
1.64 Development of techniques for handling living things correctly.
1.65 Ability to use books for supplementing ideas or information.

2.51 Knowledge of conditions which promote changes in living things and non-living materials.
2.52 Familiarity with a wide range of forces and of ways in which they can be changed.
2.53 Knowledge of sources and simple properties of common forms of energy.
2.54 Knowledge of the origins of common materials.
2.55 Awareness of some discoveries and inventions by famous scientists.
2.56 Knowledge of ways to investigate and measure properties of living things and non-living materials.
2.57 Awareness of changes in the design of measuring instruments and tools during man's history.
2.58 Skill in devising and constructing simple apparatus.
2.59 Ability to select relevant information from books or other reference material.

3.51 Knowledge that chemical change results from interaction.
3.52 Knowledge that energy can be stored and converted in various ways.
3.53 Awareness of the universal nature of gravity.
3.54 Knowledge of the main constituents and variations in the composition of soil and of the earth.
3.55 Knowledge that properties of matter can be explained by reference to its particulate nature.
3.56 Knowledge of certain properties of heat, light, sound, electrical, mechanical and chemical energy.
3.57 Knowledge of a wide range of living organisms.
3.58 Development of the concept of an internal environment.
3.59 Knowledge of the nature and variations in basic life processes.

3.61 Appreciation of levels of organisation in living things.
3.62 Appreciation of the significance of the work and ideas of some famous scientists.
3.63 Ability to apply relevant knowledge without help of contextual cues.
3.64 Ability to use scientific equipment and instruments for extending the range of human senses.

Communicating	Appreciating patterns and relationships
.70	**.80**

Stage 1
Transition from
intuition to
concrete
operations.
Infants
generally.

1.71 Ability to use new words appropriately.
1.72 Ability to record events in their sequences.
1.73 Ability to discuss and record impressions of living and non-living things in the environment.
1.74 Ability to use representational symbols for recording information on charts or block graphs.

1.81 Awareness of cause-effect relationships.

Concrete
operations.
Early stage.

1.75 Ability to tabulate information and use tables.
1.76 Familiarity with names of living things and non-living materials.
1.77 Ability to record impressions by making models, painting or drawing.

1.82 Development of a concept of environment.
1.83 Formation of a broad idea of variation in living things.
1.84 Awareness of seasonal changes in living things.
1.85 Awareness of differences in physical conditions between different parts of the Earth.

Stage 2
Concrete
operations.
Later stage.

2.71 Ability to use non-representational symbols in plans, charts, etc.
2.72 Ability to interpret observations in terms of trends and rates of change.
2.73 Ability to use histograms and other simple graphical forms for communicating data.
2.74 Ability to construct models as a means of recording observations.

2.81 Awareness of sequences of change in natural phenomena.
2.82 Awareness of structure-function relationship in parts of living things.
2.83 Appreciation of interdependence among living things.
2.84 Awareness of the impact of man's activities on other living things.
2.85 Awareness of the changes in the physical environment brought about by man's activity.
2.86 Appreciation of the relationships of parts and wholes.

Stage 3
Transition to
stage of
abstract
thinking.

3.71 Ability to select the graphical form most appropriate to the information being recorded.
3.72 Ability to use three-dimensional models or graphs for recording results.
3.73 Ability to deduce information from graphs: from gradient, area, intercept.
3.74 Ability to use analogies to explain scientific ideas and theories.

3.81 Recognition that the ratio of volume to surface area is significant.
3.82 Appreciation of the scale of the universe.
3.83 Understanding of the nature and significance of changes in living and non-living things.
3.84 Recognition that energy has many forms and is conserved when it is changed from one form to another.
3.85 Recognition of man's impact on living things—conservation, change, control.
3.86 Appreciation of the social implications of man's changing use of materials, historical and contemporary.
3.87 Appreciation of the social implications of research in science.
3.88 Appreciation of the role of science in the changing pattern of provision for human needs.

Interpreting findings critically

1.91 Awareness that the apparent size, shape and relationships of things depend on the position of the observer.

- -

1.92 Appreciation that properties of materials influence their use.

2.91 Appreciation of adaptation to environment.
2.92 Appreciation of how the form and structure of materials relate to their function and properties.
2.93 Awareness that many factors need to be considered when choosing a material for a particular use.
2.94 Recognition of the role of chance in making measurements and experiments.

3.91 Ability to draw from observations conclusions that are unbiased by preconception.
3.92 Willingness to accept factual evidence despite preceptual contradictions.
3.93 Awareness that the degree of accuracy of measurements has to be taken into account when results are interpreted.
3.94 Awareness that unstated assumptions can affect conclusions drawn from argument or experimental results.
3.95 Appreciation of the need to integrate findings into a simplifying generalisation.
3.96 Willingness to check that conclusions are consistent with further evidence.

These Stages we have chosen conform to modern ideas about children's learning. They conveniently describe for us the mental development of children between the ages of five and thirteen years, but it must be remembered that ALTHOUGH CHILDREN GO THROUGH THESE STAGES IN THE SAME ORDER THEY DO NOT GO THROUGH THEM AT THE SAME RATES.
SOME children achieve the later Stages at an early age.
SOME loiter in the early Stages for quite a time.
SOME never have the mental ability to develop to the later Stages.
ALL appear to be ragged in their movement from one Stage to another.
Our Stages, then, are not tied to chronological age, so in any one class of children there will be, almost certainly, some children at differing Stages of mental development.

Index